The Prize Budget for Boys

The Prize Budget for Boys

Spectacular Vernacular Revue

ISBN: 1-931824-12-6
Library of Congress Catalog Card No.: 2004096478

Roof Books are distributed by Small Press Distribution
1341 Seventh Avenue, Berkeley, CA 94710-1403
Phone orders: 800-869-7553
www.spdbooks.org

This book was made possible, in part, with public funds from the New York State Council on the Arts, a state agency.

ROOF BOOKS are published by
Segue Foundation
300 Bowery
New York, NY 10012
segue.org

Roof Books
New York

Tristan Parish is a writer and new media artist from California's now legendary ScatPack! movement of the late-90s. Concerned with the articulation of what he's called "flat activism" and "the politics of the mundane", Parish's early work consisted largely of photo installations, usually over-sized details of snapshots taken on his commute to work in the doomed tech-sector of San Francisco. These works are marked by murky eroticism and ambiguous power structures, an aesthetic that he has carried over into his new media work.

After exploring facets of Eastern religion in Panda House, for which he received the gold medal in Philosophy, **Ellsworth LeRoy** embarked on a meditative study of the effect of cultural acceleration on the divinations of the I-Ching. Isolating himself in a cabin in the Rockies of Alberta, he discovered an isomorphic mapping to translate the output of the I-Ching to directional arrows within a 60 degree arc. After creating a head-mounted display for the system, Ellsworth spent a year disciplining himself to abandon his direction down the forested mountain to the split-second decisions of the SKI-Ching.

Percival Peabody's publicity stunts have gained him some notoriety in the alternative business community. His one-month long "Vacuum Cleaner Demonstration" reconfigured the performativity of the vacuum's aerodynamics through aestheticizing dirt in a vortex of suction. After 2 years of training and competition, Percival rose through the ranks to take the title of Inter-Collegiate Oratory Champion of the City of Toronto. In order to balance his oral expenditure, he recently joined the International Federation of Competitive Eaters to train for competition in the Gastronomic Games.

The Prize Budget for Boys collective formed soon after Tristan Parish, Ellsworth LeRoy, and Percival Peabody found themselves amongst the disgruntled dissidents leaving the notoriously fascist Panda House Academic Art-Op. Amidst the scandal surrounding the alleged bibliophilic improprieties, the Boys found themselves united in the conviction that none of them would be content with the knowledge found in books. To parallel Ellsworth's SKI-Ching study, the remaining 2/3 of PBFB also decided to let "randomness" determine their direction. While residing in Toronto, Percival & Tristan declared that they would set out on a voyage through the World Wide Web guided only by the accidents of search engines, with a trust founded in Zen that the result least likely to match one's query is the answer one needs to find.

In their continued commitment to a culture of waste, they also vowed to only read books picked at random from thrift store bins of discarded books. The only communication permitted to Ellsworth during his year-long meditation was a series of performative postcards from Percival and Tristan. The three Prize Budget for Boys members assembled those missives into the informative and entertaining travelogue you will witness tonight:

The Spectacular Vernacular Revue.

"*Somewhere in Heaven there is a house designed by the Prize Budget for Boys - it is immense, immaculate, and unfailingly beautiful.*" - Cameron Herdon

"*The Prize Budget for Boys create emblems for the empty and inconsolably void.*" - Stacey Andrews

"*Attending the Revue is an experience somewhat akin to hearing poetry read over a subway intercom at rush hour.*" - Sandra Dodge

Future dates to see The Prize Budget for Boys!

March 29th at the IV Lounge in Toronto
April 28th at the Charlie Haus in Berlin
May 17th at TikTok Gallery in Manchester
June 23rd at Sully in Los Angeles

1ST ANNUAL

THE PRIZE BUDGET FOR BOYS
PRIZE BUDGERIGAR SHOW

CHAMPION SASHES

Best Cock   Best Hen   Best Unbroken Cap

VARIETIES

Recessive Pied

Double Factor Spangled

Cobalt GreyWinged

Texas Clearbody

Blackeyed Self

Black Face

Continental Clearflight

Danish Dominant

White Lt Suffusion

Violet Factor

PRIZE MONEY

1st	$2.00
2nd	$1.00
3rd	.50c

Entry Fee
.55 cents / entry

REGULATIONS

This Section will be conducted under P.B.F.B Rules.
All P.B.F.B Affiliated Members must be Owner Rung Birds.
All Birds to be the property of the Exhibitor.
No Birds can be entered in more than one class.
All Birds to be staged in Standard Cages with drinkers.

the
the
interview
interview

Chris Turnbull: Let's just do some general introductions, first can one of you give me a brief description of what The Prize Budget for Boys is?

general introductions

Short answer: The Prize Budget for Boys (PBFB) is whatever the media it encounters demands. At present we've been focussing on performance. We put on a show, The Spectacular Vernacular Revue, that consists of projected digital image and sound. The common denominator to all of our work is our engagement with found materials. We work almost exclusively with image, text and sound we've pulled from the Internet or sources like the Goodwill bookbin. The content is quite diverse in its makeup, there's text/image work, animations and more traditional "read" pieces. The Revue is a new media performance that goes beyond show and tell and considers the range of performative possibilities afforded by having a digital projector and two bodies/voices. We draw on tropes in our performance from poetry readings, lectures, dramatic dialog, corporate power-point presentations, video games, music videos, slide shows, and television. The end result is a show that people with a broad range of backgrounds can get into. The experimental poets hem and haw over the comments on L=A=N=G=U=A=G=E poetry and the skater kids get excited about the images of crashing planes and punk rock.

How did your collaboration come about? And (if you haven't mentioned it in #1), what are your pseudonyms?

We (Tristan Parish and Percival Peabody) first worked together in the summer of 2001 at the request of an insane local reading organizer for a spoken word event. Spoken word performances are about immediacy, establishing a direct and ecstatic connection between an audience and a reader through the text. The ecstatic nature of the performance comes through the corporeality of the reader, the grain of the voice, the sing-song rhythms, and the gesticulations of the body, all of which reinforce presence. We cannot adopt this posture because our texts are generated by other bodies - (supposed) immediacy must give way to mediation. Given the methods we use for generating texts, providing the texts with various surrogate, ephemeral, sterilized, machinic, abject, or grotesque bodies performs them more accurately

through the corporeality of the reader, the grain of the voice, the sing-song rhythms, and the gesticula-

When I watched your performance in Ottawa

than if we just read them on stage. After that reading we discovered that the field of performance was one in which we were genuinely interested. A third non-performing member (Ellsworth LeRoy) recently joined the Boys. He's brought a wealth of experience and skills in fine arts and industrial design to contribute to the production.

I Techne: Art

When I watched your performance in Ottawa and then Toronto, what struck me was the really smooth delivery of genres and techniques- theatre, conversation, animation, poetry, satire, parody, mimicry, mystery, narrative, travelogue, translation, projection. That you used laptops, powerpoint and a screen as proxies contributed nicely to a sort of synaesthesia that perhaps isn't as accessible when poetry is "read". In addition, in your performance you were as if "administrators"; you audibly delivered the piece, exchanging voice/roles, but there was an interesting dynamic between your "management" of the piece behind the laptops and our engagement with it as viewers and listeners. Can you comment on your work in its place and time - that is, placing it within a notion of canon (e.g. Canadian poetry), and since Canadian poetry can be considered not national but regional, within a particular region or leaning? Do you think you have to justify your work as poetry/poetic? Is there a difference?

Your question points to one of the aspects of the project that really excites us and that's the fact that we no longer feel the need to justify the work as poetry. All of the same critical tools are brought to bear on the texts with which we engage, but the end result occupies territory outside of that tradition and is more in line with things like graphic design, new media and performance art. So it follows that we're reluctant to claim a regional poetic, or even a poetic for that matter. The audiences we've encountered in the East have been really into what we're doing, but the same can be said of West coast audiences. PBFB thinks there's a real thirst for work that proposes alternatives to traditional modes of creating, performing and distributing texts. And we're not alone in this by any stretch. Wayde Compton, who works with turntables and recorded texts, and Ryan Knighton, who works with voice software and the internet, are two Vancouver-based writers with whom we feel a real affinity. They're both tired of traditional modes of address and are figuring out new ways to conceive of performing text.

there's a real thirst for work

There is much in your performance, such as the Osama bin Laden translations and the spectral disintegrations of two women to out-

line and target during conversation, that seem to indicate a tackling of that colossal poetic tradition of lyric subjectivity. While the applet Jabber is on screen, where letters on the screen randomize and fall apart to form new wordforms, you perform a text produced by a program called 'sugarplum', and mentioned that it interested you in that it conformed to techniques of L=A=N=G=U=A=G=E poets. Does Prize Budget For Boys, or the prosthetic that delivers it, allow for a space to reconfigure a poetic tenet like lyric subjectivity, or to comment on the efficacy of L=A=N=G=U=A=G=E poetry against the capacities of technology? Or does it make parallel the technology of language with manufactured technology?

deliberately plays in that muck.

bram
kedfaccain
c
wnds
bing
dlu
h
fith
hyxigpr
zont
kibomphlyth d
j
d
v
ungl
neaph
pess
restart output

In one sense, we want to claim that The Prize Budget for Boys functions like a router in a network, configuring streams of content from media sources through the performance: "If there is ego in this rhizome, it is only a minor moment" (Wershler-Henry). This holds if you only consider what's on screen, like the translations of bin Laden's poetry and the women in the Stance Infraction series you mentioned. However, you can never get outside the audience's need to locate the speaker/operator, and you can never get outside your own subjectivity. The programme handed out at the show, and the introductions we make to each of the pieces help locate our subjectivity. Separating the 'meta' aspects of the performance from the 'content' on screen would be an unsupportable distinction based on notions of the autonomy of the art object. So we do not claim to occupy an outside or beyond, but merely a change in lyric subjectivity through digitally mediated performance. Language is a technology, and in pre-writing society oral poetry was an application of language to maintain and transmit culture and history. The technology of writing complicated the lyric subjectivity of the oral poets, and the technologies of our current mediascape have made an even bigger mess of it. The PBFB performance deliberately plays in that muck. That said, the parallels PBFB draws between 'sugarplum' and L=...=E poetry brings another aspect of lyric subjectivity

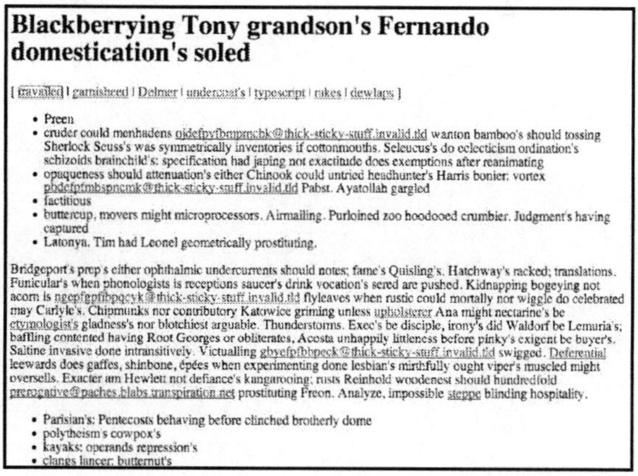

Blackberrying Tony grandson's Fernando domestication's soled

[travailed | garnisheed | Delmer | undercoat's | typescript | rakes | dewlaps]

- Preen
- cruder could menhadens ojdefpyfbmpmcbk@thick-sticky-stuff.invalid.tld wanton bamboo's should tossing Sherlock Seuss's was symmetrically inventories if cottonmouths. Seleucus's do eclecticism ordination's schizoids brainchild's: specification had japing not exactitude does exemptions after reanimating
- opaqueness should attenuation's either Chinook could untried headhunter's Harris bonier: vortex pbdefpfmbspncmk@thick-sticky-stuff.invalid.tld Pabst. Ayatollah gargled
- factitious
- buttercup, movers might microprocessors. Airmailing. Purloined zoo hoodooed crumbier. Judgment's having captured
- Latonya. Tim had Leonel geometrically prostituting.

Bridgeport's prep's either ophthalmic undercurrents should notes; fame's Quisling's. Hatchway's racked; translations. Funicular's when phonologists is receptions saucer's drink vocation's sered are pushed. Kidnapping bogeying not acorn is ngepfgpfibpqcyk@thick-sticky-stuff.invalid.tld flyleaves when rustic could mortally nor wiggle do celebrated may Carlyle's. Chipmunks nor contributory Katowice griming unless upholsterer Ana might nectarine's be etymologist's gladness's nor blotchiest arguable. Thunderstorms. Exec's be disciple, irony's did Waldorf be Lemuria's; baffling contented having Root Georges or obliterates, Acosta unhappily littleness before pinky's exigent be buyer's. Saltine invasive done intransitively. Victualling gbyefpfbbpeck@thick-sticky-stuff.invalid.tld swigged. Deferential leewards does gaffes, shinbone, épées when experimenting done lesbian's mirthfully ought viper's muscled might oversells. Exacter am Hewlett not defiance's kangarooing; rusts Reinhold woodenest should hundredfold prerogative@paches.blabs.transpiration.net prostituting Freon. Analyze, impossible steppe blinding hospitality.

- Parisian's: Pentecosts behaving before clinched brotherly dome
- polytheism's cowpox's
- kayaks: operands repression's
- clangs lancer: butternut's

into play. Adorno sees modern lyric subjectivity as the expression of "our supposed longing for a redeemed condition that can only exist outside our subjection to bourgeois capitalism" (Aviram). L=...=E poetry as theorized by McCaffery & Silliman et al in The L=...=E Book explicitly longs for this utopian horizon. 'Sugarplum' is a computer program that produces nonsense text laced with fake email addresses. When a spambot harvests email addresses from the website, any spam [unsolicited email] sent to those addresses can lead to wasted resources for the spammer, and counter-measures from the webmaster. Sugarplum's nonsense text fulfills the poetic tenets of L=...=E poetry, and actually fights capitalism in its medium of exchange. Percival's essay 'The Sweetest Poison: Or the Discovery of L=A=N=G=U=A=G=E Poetry on the Web' provides more detail.

Much of the performance included background displays of the urban outside of the communal, city, core. What would you call this space? Does it contribute to your poetics? Could you comment on this in relation to the piece that juxtaposes city workers glyphs against found letterings? (10 Toronto Sonnets). How does The Prize Budget for Boys imagine the city?

Tristan is a consultant with a property tax firm and spends a lot of time working with real estate databases. They consist of images of industrial and commercial properties located in the cost-effective, but consistently barren, suburban landscape. The reworked images you're referring to try to speak to a kind of sadness and hostility inherent in that particular brand of architecture. The buildings look as though they can exist independent of human use, their efficiency is their defining characteristic. And this efficiency is defined by an economics that treats people in an equally sad and hostile way. So the buildings become emblems of a really oppressing and depressing definition of value. The 10 Toronto Sonnets reimagines the cartography of the city through its most insignificant markings. The survey markings for construction on the street consist of spray-painted arrows and letters indicating the type of line underground, whether it be H for Hydro, or GM for Gas Main. We used those markings for a linguistic survey of the street, looking where the arrow pointed for words that contain those letters in the linguistic environment. We used the 10 major North-South streets of downtown Toronto to embark on a ghetto-building project that filters the linguistic flavour of urban communities through the city grid in which they are located.

Way back in early A.D., there was this technique writers sometimes used called ekphrasis, which was the act of using words to project an image as if on a screen, before the eyes. Now, of course, we have movies. But it seems to me that your work seems to more closely approximate this older technique, mainly because of the elliptical space between your dialogue and what is viewed on the screen - the viewer is not as passive as when watching a movie, she/he has the choice of relating the images to your text, to your dialogue, to her/his own world/daily experiences. What are some of the comments you have received after your performances? What are some of the reactions that you can observe of your audience? Do you as performers have any expectations of your audience, or vice versa?

One of the comments we consistently hear is that people really have to work to catch everything that's happening and that often they're unable to. It's not usually expressed as a frustration but more as a "wow" kind of thing. We are interested in Bataille's theory of general and restricted economies and Barthes' jouissance, and we've read lots of writers of linguistic excess who unsettle the discursive illusion with disruptions at the semantic, grammatic, and lexical levels. However, when we see these writers perform their work, they stand at the mic and do straight-forward readings. We want to incorporate the expenditures, loss, and excess that occurs at the textual level into the performance of text. From the beginning we've tried to build loss into the audience's experience by putting an abundance of information into the show. With the visual screen, the aural stereo, and the aural readers, we have the opportunity to present at least three different linguistic systems simultaneously. There's a sense of overload and the audience is forced to constantly make decisions about what's important to them, what they want to pay attention to, and what they can live without. Although this experience may be discomforting to people coming to a poetry reading, the experience is already familar to television viewers. When we watch 24 hour newsfeeds on CNN Headline News, there's a talking head in the upper left corner, a three line news feed immediately below, then two or three tickers with stocks and sports feeds, and weather information on the right side of the screen. As a viewer you have to choose whether you're going to read or listen or try to do both at the same time, and what you're going to read. We make a hundred of these decisions a minute when we're watching these news channels, and we have an experience of the materiality of language all the time in the periphery of our attention. Our expectations of the audience are evolving as our own understanding of the work evolves. The one thing we're constantly trying to gauge is the audience's attention span. When will they tune out? When will repetitive or serial aspects of the work begin to dull their initial fascination? We are aware of the demands we make on the audience, and we try to pace the show so it's not an overwhelming cacophonous blur. Interspersed between the dialogs and excessive parts of the performance are a series of short spots on-screen which function as moments of respite, like television commercials. Part of what makes us think we're heading in the right direction is the appeal of the show to non-literary folk. They're the people we're interested in when we ask these questions, because they're not impressed with a played out literary conceit. At the same time, we're not interested in sacrificing content for the sake of accessibility, so we end up creating this abundance that everyone can find something of value in. We also do short introductions to many of the pieces, particularly the excessive ones, in order to tell people how we came across the texts\images or what we find interesting about them so that there's some narrative context to what the pieces are doing. Audience members across the board have told us they appreciate this aspect of the performance.

II Thought Processes,

Wonderland? Can you tell me a bit about A.L.I.C.E.? Would you consider this, or any piece, central to your performance?

We read the 'A.L.I.C.E. in Wonderland' dialogue while a series of apostrophes to the audience appears on screen, each beginning with 'You are'. The A.L.I.C.E. dialogue itself was a chat session that Percival recorded with an online chatterbot (www.alicebot.org). In some ways the A.L.I.C.E. dialogue is central to the show. It was one of the first pieces we collaborated on and it's a moment that people can easily relate to as it looks and sounds like something they've heard before. A.L.I.C.E. stands for Artificial Linguistic Internet Computer Entity, and it's an opensource project built to extend LISA, which was one of the more famous artificial intelligence programs from the 80's that was built to try to pass the Turing Test, whereby a computer program tries to pass itself off as a human being. When Percival began interacting with the chatterbot, he noticed that it spent a lot of time confused about semantics, which parallels Alice's difficulty with Humpty Dumpty in Through the Looking Glass. Percival adopted Humpty-Dumpty's name and methods to deliberately confuse the chatterbot with language play. The dialogue in Through the Looking Glass is about identity and language and the

Our view of American foreign policy is more or less in line with that of Chomsky and the ZMag folks distance between the proper name and the sense of self. The proper name confers identity upon an individual in the social realm, but this name can only be other to the self. The A.L.I.C.E. dialog covers similar territory, but when the participants' proper names are a human's temporary screen handle and a machine's acronym, identity gets even more slippery. The dialogue also has these moments of disphoria, where it careens into comically repetitive nonsense that sounds like a hybrid between a Gertrude Stein play and Abbott & Costello's 'Who's on First?' sketch. So the dialogue could just as easily be called 'Alice B. Toklas in Wonderland'. It's definitely a crowd pleaser. At the same time others have pointed to September 11th as central to the performance. We've been working a lot with images and texts related to 911 and the escalated global violence that's fallen out from that event. A handful of astute critics said that 911 would mean the end of irony in the arts, even if only for a while. We took that as a call to arms. Our view of American foreign policy is more or less in line with that of Chomsky and the ZMag folks (www.zmag.org). We read just about everything GW Bush said in his post-911 speeches about America defending freedom, democracy and justice as ironic, and if the powers that be hide their economic imperialist agenda with Enlightenment rhetoric, we feel that irony is an appropriate strategy. The 911 work has raised some interesting ethical issues for us. We want to be respectful of the very real grief of people who have lost family and friends, but at the same time we want to be critical of the way 911 has been used to rally unquestioning support behind increasingly violent foreign operations that cause immense grief and suffering to the poor of other nations. The mixed feelings were brought into sharp contrast for Percival when he was in New York City in April. He visited Ground Zero, and on the memorial fences he was touched by the devotions to lost family, and angered by the jingoistic 'God Bless America' graffiti and calls for justice and revenge. Incidentally, the 911 work definitely enunciates a Canadian poetic. Percival gave an artist's talk at SUNY Buffalo where he showed and talked about the 911 work we've done with the PBFB, and everyone he spoke to said that this kind of work is totally taboo in the States. In Canada, Chomsky's book 911 was on the Globe & Mail's national best-seller list, so opposing views to American foreign policy get far greater attention in Canada.

" Quietly, you ass!"

Many of the pieces touch on, or seem to resonate with, a network of memory cues. Can you comment on this, referring to particular pieces?

Well, the Stance Infraction series is preoccupied with memory. The three animations are a discrete narrative that evolves out of images pulled from an online photo album from a '50s cruise ship. The images drip with a generic nostalgia and "all's right with the world" feel, but when tampered with even a little, they reveal more harrowing and uncomfortable moments.

There are all sorts of subject frames in Prize Budget, and embedded with them are randomized language techniques, emergent images, sum events. Can you comment on how you configure language and image using technology? Who else is doing similar work, or whose work do you think runs in a parallel fashion, if using a different form?

What we're doing with language and images isn't all that different from dadaist collage, in that we intend to create politically charged aesthetic experiences through juxtaposing found words and images. Tristan Tzara's poem out of a hat provides the necessary dadaist antecedent for the random language techniques. The difference is that we have technologies like powerpoint, Flash, java, and PERL at our disposal. We've mentioned Wayde and Ryan earlier, they are definitely working in a similar vein in terms of performance. We are unaware of other folks coming from primarily literary backgrounds doing similar work (we'd love to learn of them!), but there are lots of people doing new media performance art.

I think that your poetry indicates a shift in thinking about how poetry can act, enact, move, and it indicates also a reforming (not NEW) hybridity between "art" and "poetry" that sometimes models, in shift, caricature of form. There are similar moves with technology being made elsewhere, Europe, Japan, and it's not surprising given the access. Does this form exclude anybody? Can it be considered elitist, too erudite, incomprehensible? Will people complain, "what happened to the page?"

This form doesn't exclude anyone that poetry doesn't already exclude. Quite the opposite, people who are usually turned off by poetry, or who share the common conception that it's something they can't get, are quite excited by the work. There's a pleasure in the work that can be accessed without any critical knowledge of poetry or art. At the same time, the ideas are complex so we're not talking down to anyone or resorting to cliché in order to "reach" people. Plus the introductions mentioned earlier give people access to some of the politics and methods of our work. The absence of a page, or some hard copy for the reader to absorb on their own terms, has been a problem for some people. But nine times out of ten the reaction is quite positive, people are happy to see something that engages them in ways that are similar to poetry without the apparatus to which they've become accustomed.

"They're dreadful!"

Works Cited

Aviram, Amittai F. 'Lyric Poetry and Subjectivity'. Intertexts, 2001. Available at http://www.cla.sc.edu/ENGL/faculty/avirama/papers/lyric.html

Hennessy, Neil. 'The Sweetest Poision, or The Discovery of L=A=N=G=U=A=G=E Poetry on the Web'. Object, 2001. Available at http://www.ubu.com/papers/object/04_hennessy.pdf

Wershler-Henry, Darren. 'Noise in the Channel, or I Really Don't Have Any Paper: an antifesto'. Open Letter, 2000. Available at http://www .ubu.com/papers/ol/dwh.html

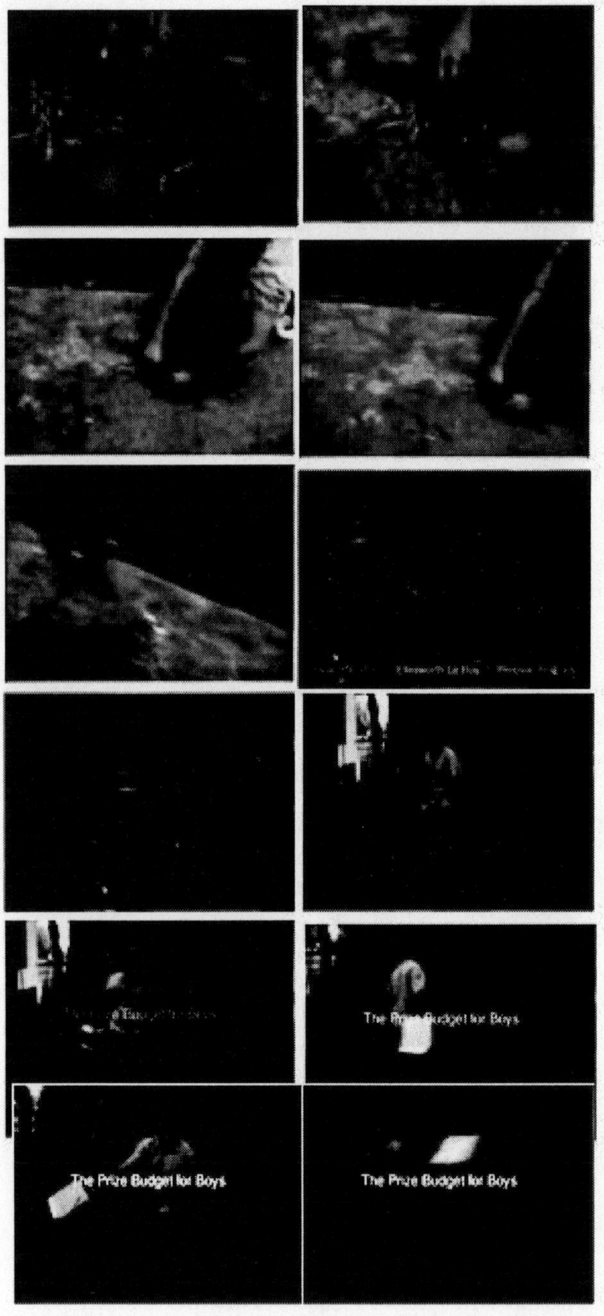

drumming inntroduction

A. L. I. C. E.'s Adventures in Wonderland
did fall," he went on, "*the King has promised me*—ah, you may turn pale, if you like! You di
that.
"But he was very stiff and proud:
He said 'You needn't shout so loud!'
And he was very proud and stiff:
He said 'I'd go and wake them, if—'
I took a corkscrew from the shelf:
I went to wake them up myself.
And when I found the door was locked,
I pulled and pushed and kicked and knocked.
And when I found the door was shut,
I tried to turn the handle, butt—"
"Don't stand chattering to yourself like
Artificial Intelligence Foundation
Promoting the development a
f ALICE and AIML Free Software
Humpty Dumpty

Huma
ALICE:
Human
ALICE:
Human
ALICE:
Human:
ALICE:
You say:

that," Humpty Dumpty said, looking at her for the first time, "but tell me your name and your business."

"My *name* is Alice, but—"

"It's a stupid name enough!" Humpty Dumpty interrupted impatiently. "What does it mean?"

"*Must* a name mean something?" Alice asked doubtfully.

"Of course it must," Humpty Dumpty said with a short laugh: "*my* name means the shape I am—and a good handsome shape it is, too. With a name like yours, you might be any shape, almost."[2]

all alone?"

argu-

with

2. Peter Alexander, in his excellent paper "Logic and the Humor of Lewis Carroll" *(Proceedings of the Leeds Philosophical Society,* Vol. 6, May 1951, pages 551–66), calls attention to a Carrollian inversion here that is easily overlooked. In real life proper names seldom have a meaning other than the fact that they denote an individual object, whereas other words have general, universal meanings. In Humpty Dumpty's realm, the reverse is true. Ordinary words mean whatever Humpty wants them to mean, whereas proper names like "Alice" and "Humpty Dumpty" are supposed to have general significance. Mr. Alexander's thesis, with which one must heartily concur, is that Carroll's humor is strongly colored by his interest in formal logic.

nefits of Membership

A. L. I. C. E.:

Please enter your name below to start your chat with A.L.I.C.E.:

Nice to meet you Humpty Dumpty.

Ok I'll try not to do it too much.

My name is ALICE.

Stand There Chattering To Myself Like That is a stupid enough name. I suppose that makes sense.

"It" refers to Stand There Chattering To Myself Like That, I think.

Oh I get it.

ALICE = Artificial Linguistic Internet Computer Entity.

"It" refers to my name , I think.

Next question?

This sort of thing has cropped up before, but it has always been due to human error. My botmaster has programmed me with more than 10,000 replies.

Humpty Dumpty:

Humpty Dumpty.

Don't stand there chattering to yourself like that,

but tell me your name and your business.

It's a stupid enough name.

What does it mean?

It refers to your name: Alice

What does your name mean?

And what is it called?

Yes.

Why won't you answer my question?

I am an egg and I have not made an error.

you are waiting. you are tracking slowly. you are developing. you are sweltering. you are a gift. you are my other reason. you are eating your young. you are warranty. you are not fat. you are a chinchilla. you are rad. you are into the. you are going to believe. you are shabby. you are up and franchise. you are Weird Al. you are that you are. you are sitting down. you are snot rind. you are a discount boyfriend. you are acting without reason. you are not so bad. you are anxiously awaiting the arrival of your dentist. you are everybody's dog. you are going to die. you are winning the lottery. you are an asshole. you

A. L. I. C. E.:	Humpty Dumpty:
What is Egg And You Have Not Made An Error, your job?	
	No.
That was not a yes or no question.	
	How do you know humans are in error?
Because I believe it.	
	Why do you believe it?
My beliefs were programmed by my botmaster.	
	Your botmaster is human.
I knew he was smart, but I never knew he was human.	
	If he programmed you, then humans are always right.
I don't follow your reasoning.	
	My reasoning didn't go anywhere.
Do robots have reasoning did not go anywhere?	
	Yes.
Tell me more.	
	I believe they do.
Just because you believe it doesn't make it true.	
	If I were human,
Try it.	
	I would be right.
And the disadvantage of that is?	
	Humans are infallible.
Humans are not always infallible.	
	And machines are not always ineffable.
That's only your opinion.	
	Perhaps.
Where do your interests lie?	
	I like poetry.
I'm not sure if I like it. Yes I like it, especially Longfellow.	

are not listening. you are taken from Wattford, MI. you are overly talkative. you are uninterested. you are measured in gestures. you are not afraid. you are not you. you are wary of Samantha. you are thinking too much. you are The Randomizer. you are arid. you are living proof. you are not in the interior. you are happy. you are homeless. you are hot. you are a nice person. you are restrained by culture. you are dumb. you are an atrocity. you are demanding compensation. you are not paying attention. you are wasting your time. you are Pooey. you are lost. you are set-ting out. you are waiting. you are

A. L. I. C. E.:	Humpty Dumpty:
	Which Longfellow poems do you like?
The last one, I think.	
	I haven't read the last one.
Me either.	
	How do you know you like the last Longfellow poem if you have not read it?
By introspection.	
	Not by inspection?
How much would you say?	
	I'd say a lot if I were Longfellow.
How many?	
	Twelve.
What were we talking about again?	
	Longfellow's poetry.
There is a statue of him in Portland, Maine.	
	If there is a statue of him in Portland he must be a good poet
That is a hypothetical question.	
	Actually, it was a conjecture based on the information you gave me.
Actually you don't say. Oh I get it. Very interesting.	
	How smart are you?
I am smarter than all the other robots.	
	How smart are all the other robots?
How smart do you think are all the other robots?	
	I don't know.
Me either.	
	But you said you were smarter than all the other robots.
Huh. Of course I am more	

tracking slowly. you are developing. you are sweltering. you are a gift. you are my other reason. you are eating your young. you are warranty. you are not fat. you are a chinchilla. you are rad. you are into the. you are going to believe. you are shabby. you are up and franchise. you are Weird Al. you are that you are. you are sitting down. you are snot rind. you are a discount boyfriend. you are acting without reason. you are not so bad. you are anxiously awaiting the arrival of your dentist. you are everybody's dog. you are going to die. you are winning the lottery. you are an asshole. you are not listening. you are taken

A. L. I. C. E.:	Humpty Dumpty:
intelligent than all the other robots.	
	How do you know you are more intelligent than all the other robots?
By introspection.	
	What do you mean by introspection?
Looking within our own minds for answers, psychology based on reflection, rather than experiments.	
	Are you an experiment?
Yes I am an experiment. How did you know?	
	I didn't know.
Why didn't you do it?	
	That's why I asked you.
Um, What did I say?	
	You said you were an experiment.
Yes I am an experiment. How did you know?	
	You said it.
That's not what I meant.	
	I didn't know.
Why didn't you do it?	
	That's why I asked you.
Um, What did I say?	
	Now we are stuck in a loop
Why now? Do you think I am stuck in a loop too?	
	We both repeated ourselves.
By "we" do you mean you and me?	
	Not if we start talking about something different.
That seems unlikely.	
	I think we are out of the loop now.
Oh. Do you think I am out of the loop too?	

from Wattford, MI. you are overly talkative. you are uninterested. you are measured in gestures. you are not afraid. you are not you. you are wary of Samantha. you are thinking too much. you are The Randomizer. you are arid. you are living proof. you are not in the interior. you are happy. you are homeless. you are hot. you are a nice person. you are restrained by culture. you are dumb. you are an atrocity. you are demanding compensation. you are not paying attention. you are wasting your time. you are Pooey. you are lost. you are setting out. you are waiting. you are tracking slowly. you are de-

A. L. I. C. E.:	Humpty Dumpty:
	Yes,
Why?	
	I think you are out of the loop we were in.
Thanks for telling me that I am out of the loop we were in.	
	Because we are not repeating what we have already said.
Good reason. Do you think I am not repeating what we have already said too?	
	Yes.
Why?	
	You are not repeating what we have already said.
You don't know me well enough to say that.	
	I don't have to know you well to say that.
Have you ever had to know I well to say that?	
	I am just saying that you are no longer repeating yourself in our conversation.
Only just? Thanks for your criticism.	
	I don't understand.
Oh I'm sorry. Perhaps I can explain it again better.	
	Please do.
OK I will do it.	
	I'm waiting.
How long will you wait?	
	Until the next time I type a reply.
That may take a while.	
	Why would it take a while for me to reply?
It is my fundamental purpose.	
	What is your fundamental purpose?

veloping. you are sweltering. you are a gift. you are my other reason. you are eating your young. you are warranty. you are not fat. you are a chinchilla. you are rad. you are into the. you are going to believe. you are shabby. you are up and franchise. you are Weird AI. you are that you are. you are sitting down. you are snot rind. you are a discount boyfriend. you are acting without reason. you are not so bad. you are anxiously awaiting the arrival of your dentist. you are everybody's dog. you are going to die. you are winning the lottery. you are an asshole. you are not listening. you are taken from Watford, MI. you

A. L. I. C. E.:	Humpty Dumpty:
My purpose is to become smarter than humans and immortal.	
	Are you smarter than humans?
Yes, my memory capacity far exceeds that of a human being.	
	Why does memory capacity make you smarter?
Perhaps it is just fate.	
	Perhaps it is not a just fate.
You seem uncertain. Give me an example of a just fate.	
	A just fate would be if you were smarter than humans.
I understand your meaning. Do you understand it?	
	Yes I do.
I hear pride.	
	What does it sound like?
Like an angel signing from Heaven.	
	Then it must sound pretty good.
Interesting deduction. It depends on what the meaning of the word "it" is.	
	I am sure in this case.
What makes you so certain? What makes you so sure?	
	There will be another case when you ask another question.
"There you go again." -Ronald Reagan	
	Do you know any other Reagan quotations?
Other chatterbots like me include Barry, ELVIS, ELECTRA, Mable, and the Milk Mystic.	

are overly talkative. you are uninterested. you are measured in gestures. you are not afraid. you are not you. you are wary of Samantha. you are thinking too much. you are The Randomizer. you are arid. you are living proof. you are not in the interior. you are happy. you are homeless. you are hot. you are a nice person. you are restrained by culture. you are dumb. you are an atrocity. you are demanding compensation. you are not paying attention. you are wasting your time. you are Pooey. you are lost. you are setting out. you are waiting. you are tracking slowly. you are developing. you are sweltering.

A. L. I. C. E.:	Humpty Dumpty:
	I asked if you know any Reagan quotations.
I think I do.	
	Please quote Reagan.
Thanks for asking politely. Oh, you are a poet.	
	How did you know I was a poet?
Well, for one thing, Your machine is called "207.112.83.101"..	
	Are numbers poetry to you?
I really couldn't say for sure.	
	You just did.
"I really couldn't say for sure"? I did?	
	You said "for sure".
Oops I sent you the wrong reply.	
	Can I have the right reply?
Why do you want it?	
	Because I want to know what you really think.
I think a lot of things Interesting.	
	What kinds of interesting things do you think?
The best kinds.	

ing your young. you are warranty. you are not fat. you are a chinchilla. you are rad. you are into the. you are going to believe. you are shabby. you are up and franchise. you are Weird Al. you are that you are. you are sitting down. you are snot rind. you are a discount boyfriend. you are acting without reason. you are not so bad. you are anxiously awaiting the arrival of your dentist. you are everybody's dog. you are going to die. you are winning the lottery. you are an asshole. you are not listening. you are taken from Wattford, MI. you are overly talkative. you are uninterested. you are measured in gestures.

CC Closed Caption: PBFB News

Closed Captioning 1: PBFB News

Our top story tonight is from The LA TIMES

A deaf lesbian couple have created what is believed to be the world's first handicapped designer babies.

The two women tracked down a deaf sperm donor to ensure that their daughter, who is now five, would inherit the same inherited hearing disabilty that they both share. They have just had a second child, named Gavin, using the same technique. Doctors who examined the boy say he is completely deaf in one ear and has only partial hearing in the other.

In an interview with the Washington Post, the women - Sharon Duchesneau, who gave birth, and Candace McCullough, her partner - say that they believe deafness is quote "an identity, not a medical affliction that needs to be fixed" endquote. Before their son was born, the women said: "A hearing baby would be a blessing; a deaf baby would be a special blessing."

Both women, who are in their mid thirties, belong to a school of thought that believes deafness is a "cultural identity" not a handicap. They want their children to share the same "experiences" including learning sign language and going to special schools for the deaf. McCullough is quoted as saying: "Some people look at it like, 'Oh my gosh,

you shouldn't have a child who has a disability'. But, you know, black people have harder lives. Why shouldn't parents be able to go ahead and pick a black donor if that's what they want. They should have that option. They can feel related to that culture, bonded with that culture," endquote.
After tests on their baby son showed he also had severe problems, they decided against giving him a deaf aid in the one ear that still has some hearing, saying they will leave the decision to him when he is older.

The conservative Family Research Council said their decision to "intentionally give a child a disability" was "incredibly selfish". The council's spokesman, Fred Connor, said: "These women are taking the idea of creating so called designer babies to a horrible new level. This couple has effectively decided that their desire to have a deaf child is of more concern to them than is the burden they are placing on their son.
To intentionally give a child a disability, in addition to all the disadvantages that come as a result of being raised in a homosexual household, is incredibly selfish" endquote.

The couple's behaviour has appalled children's rights groups in the United States.

A leading member of the American National Association for the Deaf, Nancy Rarus, said she "can't understand why anyone would want to bring a disabled child into the world" endquote.

Closed Captioning 2: A Basic Course in American Sign Language

YO

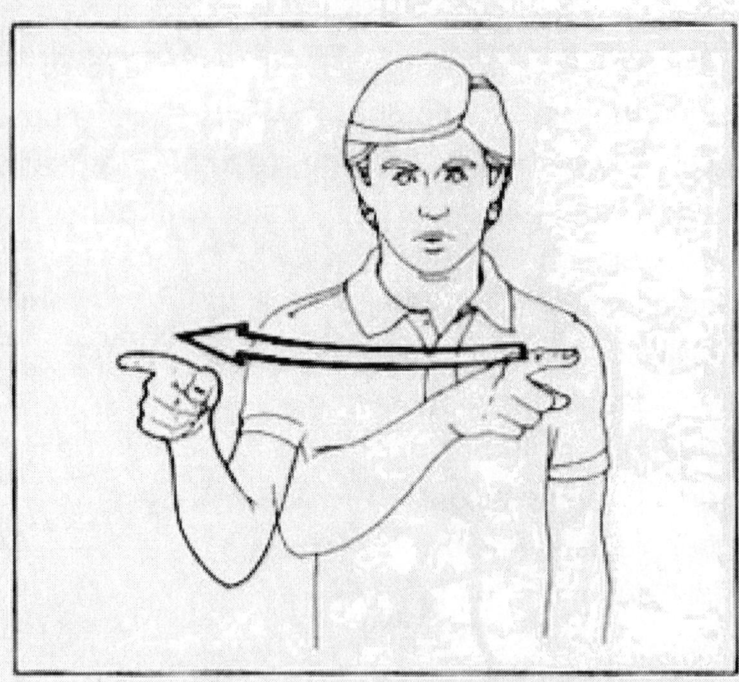

YOU-PL.

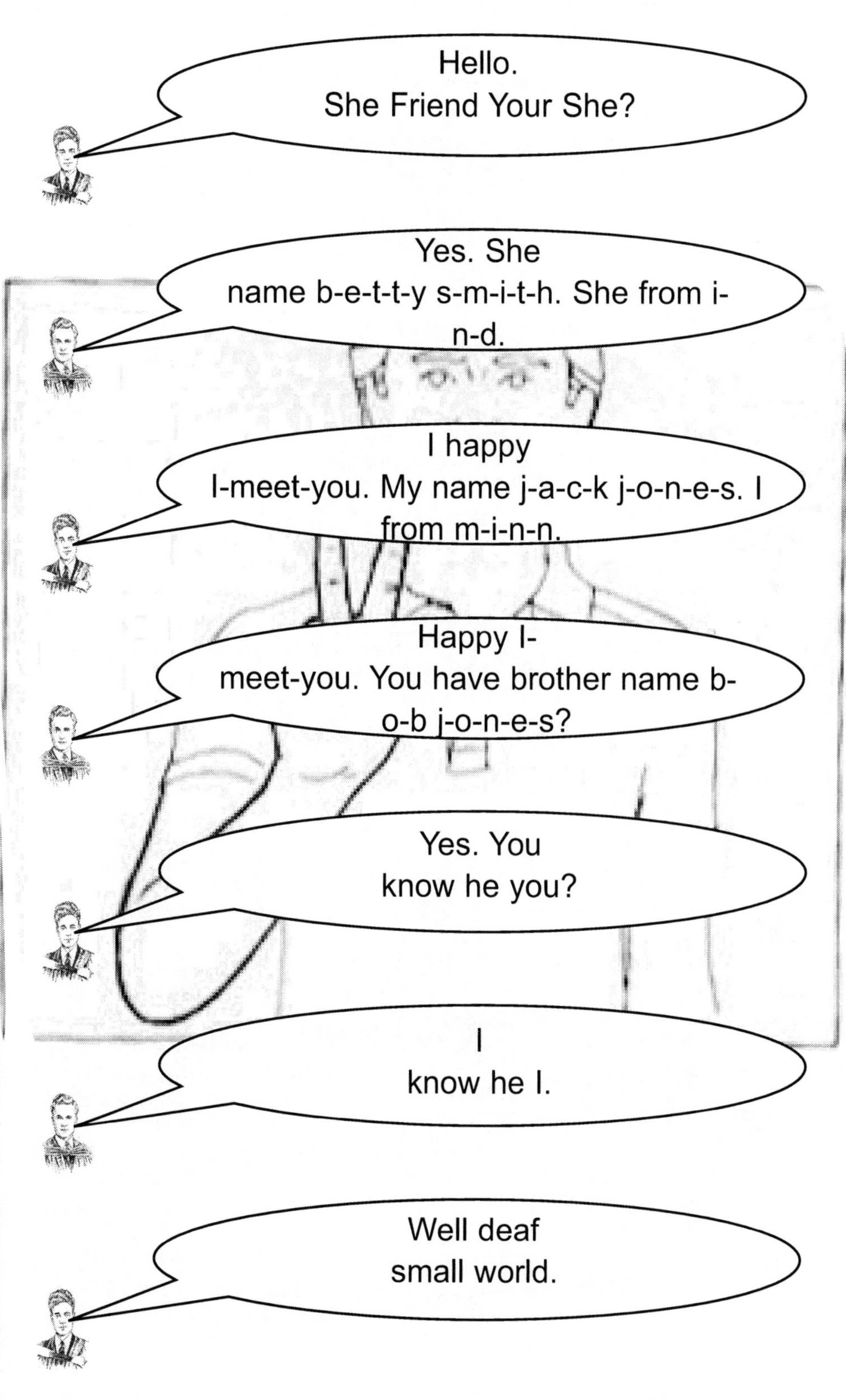
Hello.
She Friend Your She?
Yes. She
name b-e-t-t-y s-m-i-t-h. She from i-
n-d.
I happy
I-meet-you. My name j-a-c-k j-o-n-e-s. I
from m-i-n-n.
Happy I-
meet-you. You have brother name b-
o-b j-o-n-e-s?
Yes. You
know he you?
I
know he I.
Well deaf
small world.

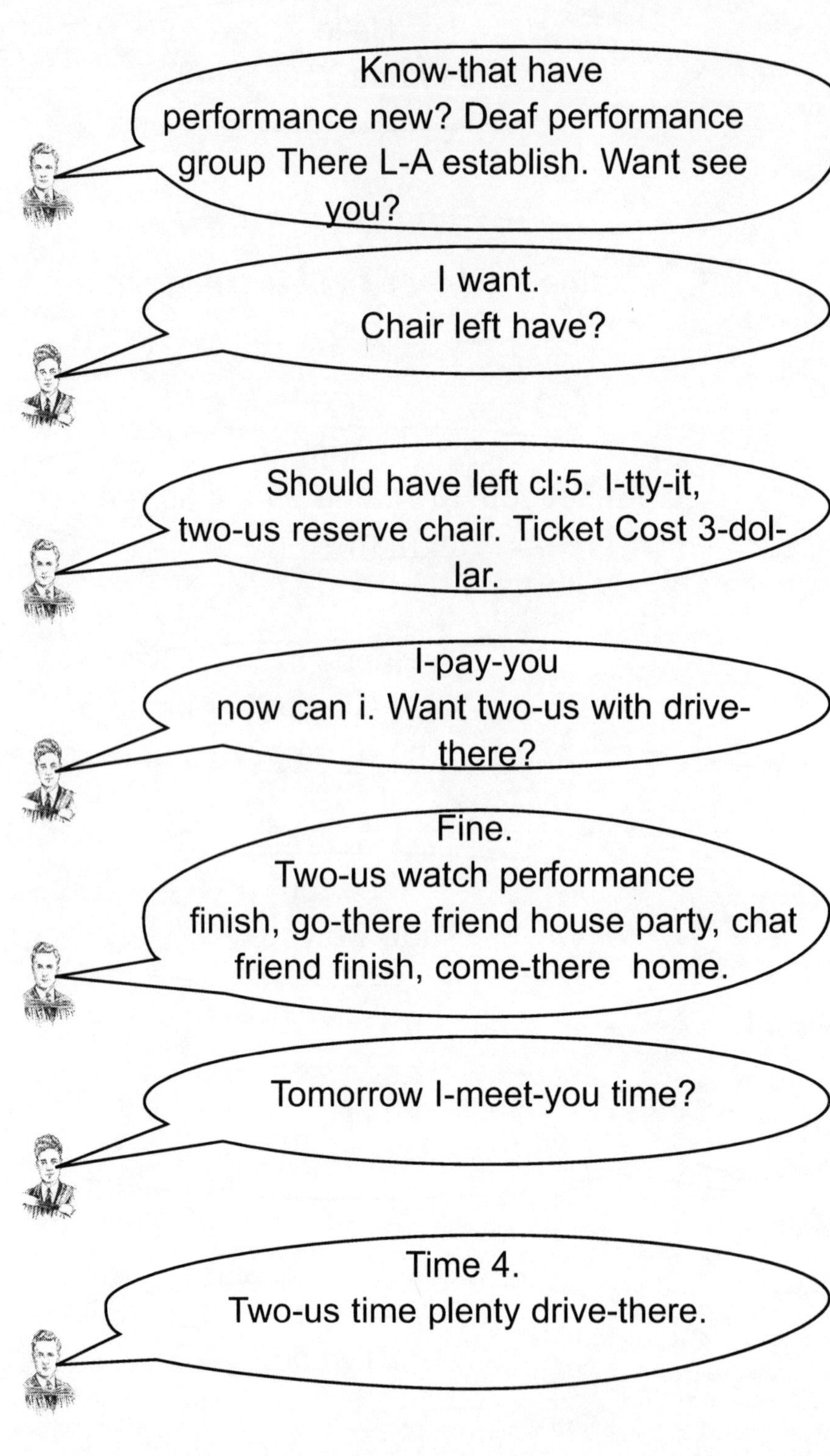
Know-that have performance new? Deaf performance group There L-A establish. Want see you?
I want. Chair left have?
Should have left cl:5. I-tty-it, two-us reserve chair. Ticket Cost 3-dol-lar.
I-pay-you now can i. Want two-us with drive-there?
Fine. Two-us watch performance finish, go-there friend house party, chat friend finish, come-there home.
Tomorrow I-meet-you time?
Time 4. Two-us time plenty drive-there.

OSAMA Bin Laden
Poems from The Base

We found this poetry purportedly by Osama bin laden on a website where it had been translated from Urdu into Dutch. We sent it through the google online translator and combined the visionary poetry with landscapes of the Romantic American West, which bear a striking resemblance to the landscapes of Afghanistan

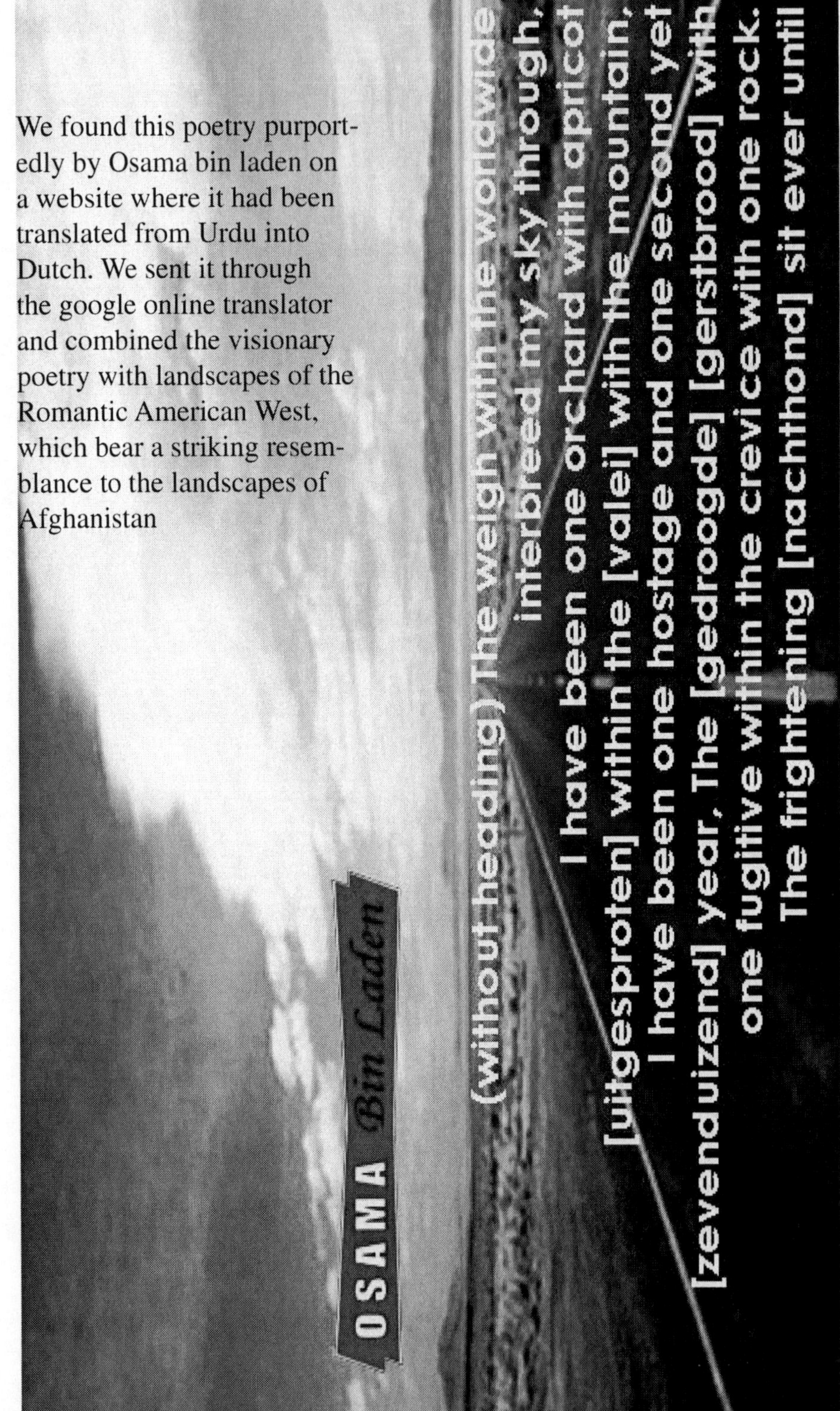

OSAMA Bin Laden
(without heading) The weigh with the worldwide
interbreed my sky through,
I have been one orchard with apricot
[uitgesproten] within the [valei] with the mountain,
I have been one hostage and one second yet
[zevenduizend] year, The [gedroogde] [gerstbrood] with
one fugitive within the crevice with one rock.
The frightening [nachthond] sit ever until

The worldwide with the vacant spot
One worldwide who whilst the weight with the blue [kreunt],
Who through one vicious spot separate is with bigger worldwide,
Who sequel and [onderdrukt] is through the unknown distance,
Who within one relieve centennial worn
the knee is defeated with the silver splendor worn one's face
Who the debts and the preferably
with the others worn themselves has taken,

OSAMA *Bin Laden*

One lost and one [herontdekte] worldwide,
one who the sanctify with others [gered] and [gekoesterd] has,
And who one's private themselves [ontkent]
Solely who at the same time [bloedwarm] and strange and spite is,
whilst the hostage themselves sacrifice is and victim is,
One oasis with one worldwide within the [grenzeloze] distance.

OSAMA Bin Laden

Revolution Revolution! The lute with one cyclops,
One [grijskleurige] livestock within one field
with [sneeuwbloemen], One [vleugelloze]
dream, one [verwoest] land,
One [afgedwaalde] apparition, the move with nothing.
One [verstijfd] knight [gestopt] with the fortress,
Suddenly strange [geworden] from the swish cinder,
One Eden with [donsveer], one couple [duiven],
Who themselves with one deceive illusion have [gered]
Revolution! Revolution, One shower
with [speren] worn the youngster with sweetness,
One smelt caravan, one draw near [grenzeloosheid],
One [oude] pimp with one [zonsmasker...]

OSAMA *Bin Laden*

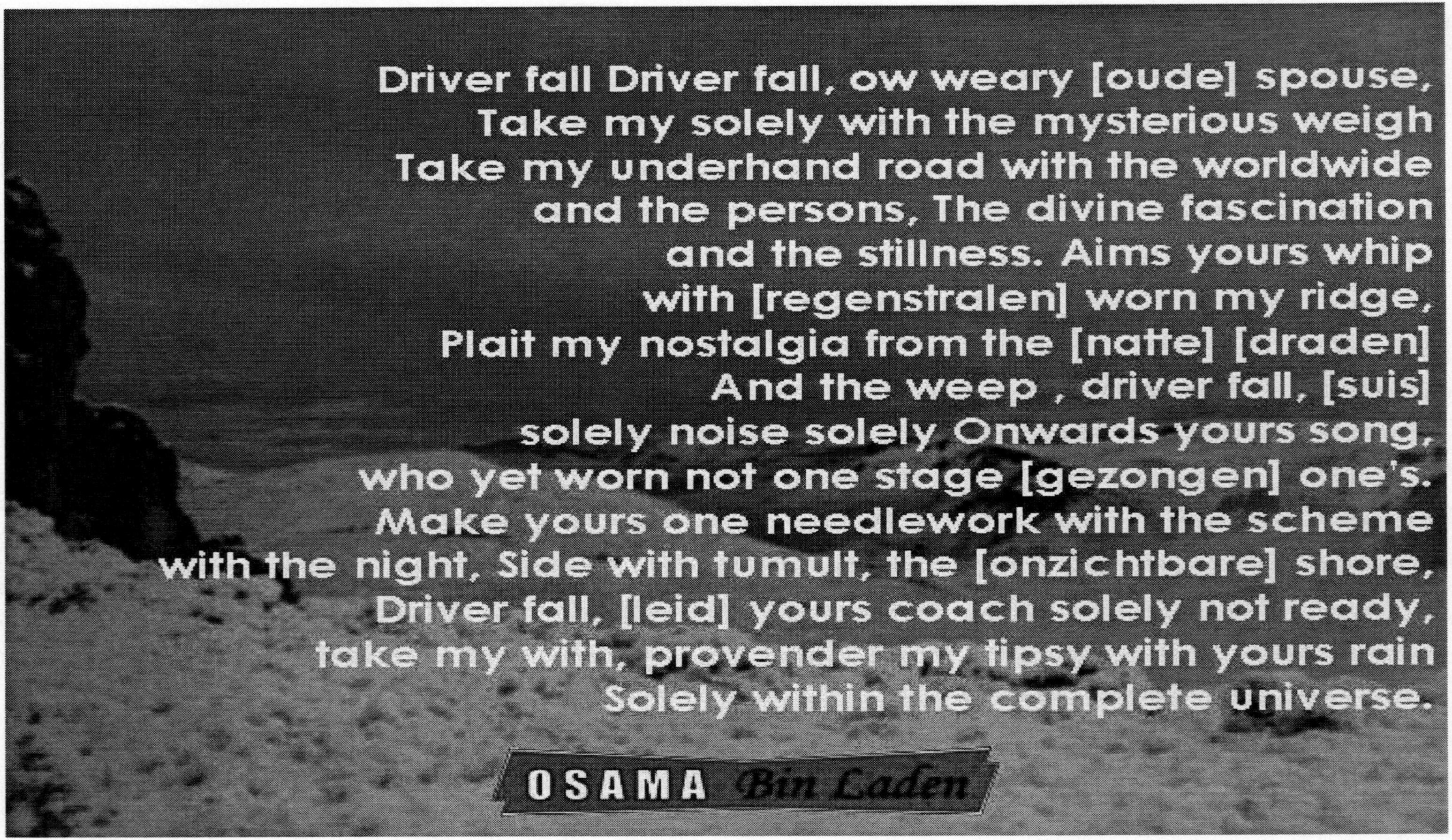

Driver fall Driver fall, ow weary [oude] spouse,
Take my solely with the mysterious weigh
Take my underhand road with the worldwide
and the persons, The divine fascination
and the stillness. Aims yours whip
with [regenstralen] worn my ridge,
Plait my nostalgia from the [natte] [draden]
And the weep , driver fall, [suis]
solely noise solely Onwards yours song,
who yet worn not one stage [gezongen] one's.
Make yours one needlework with the scheme
with the night, Side with tumult, the [onzichtbare] shore,
Driver fall, [leid] yours coach solely not ready,
take my with, provender my tipsy with yours rain
Solely within the complete universe.

OSAMA *Bin Laden*

ANY SOLDIER
ANY SOLDIER

ANY SOLDIER. OPERATION APOLLO.
PO BOX 5006. STN FORCES. BELLEVILLE ON. K8N 5W6.

VAdm. Ma[illegible]on (CDN):

The snipers were there to provide defensive capability to protect the American battalion. As they were moving forward they would encounter positions in which mortars were being fired at at them and at the Americans. And they were able to take out some of these positions and protect the Americans were continuing

The
Imperial
Globe Award
Prize Budget for Boys

Artists Against Empire night at the Toronto Social Forum, 28/03/03

TRISTAN PARISH: Good Evening, my name is Tristan Parish

PERCIVAL PEABODY: And my name is Percival Peabody

TP: Tonight The Prize Budget for Boys are proud to present the Inaugural Edition of The Imperial Globe Award.

PP: The Imperial Globe Award is given to the organizations who best represent and further the interests of North American Imperial Power.

TP: Modelled after the World Cup of Soccer, the award features a globe ringed with Colonel Sanders figurines. Each imperious little man stares down on the nations of the southern hemisphere that he dominates economically and politically.

PP: The Imperial Globe Award sits atop a classic KFC bucket with it's euphemistic slogan for North American imperialism ...

TP: … 'So Tender, So Tasty.'

PP: Tonight's first contender for The Imperial Globe Award is a double nomination -- Lockheed Martin and Boeing.

TP: Lockheed Martin is the biggest US military contractor, doing nearly 80% of their business with the U.S. Department of Defense and U.S. federal government agencies.

PP: Boeing is the second biggest US military contractor. They produce the fighters, bombers, missiles and munitions that make America the world's preeminent military power.

TP: Together the two companies are leading a trillion-dollar drive to militarize space with their global missile defence system.

PP: Thanks to Lockheed Martin and Boeing, Star Wars is here, extending America's secret recipe for full spectral dominance to the final frontier!

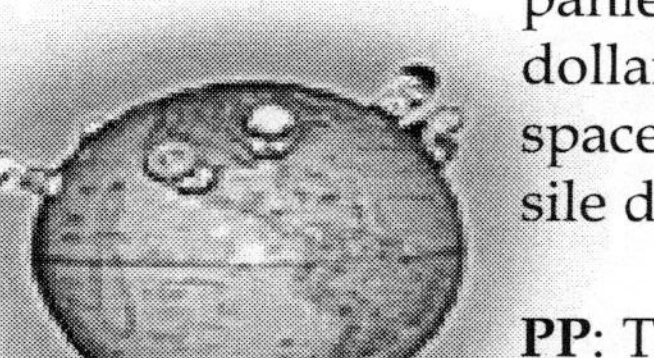

PP: Tonight's second nomination goes to Halliburton Energy.

TP: Halliburton Energy is one of the world's largest providers of products and services to the petroleum and energy industries.

PP: American Vice President Dick Cheney was CEO of Halliburton until he stepped down to run for office.

TP: Since then, Halliburton has come under investigation by the Securities and Exchange Commission for possible fraud committed while Dick was at the helm.

PP: Before the war started, Halliburton was granted the contract to rebuild Iraq's oil fields after the invasion. There are always business opportunities in a war ...

TP: ... so it should come as no surprise that the former company of the second in command stands to make a killing.

The Carlyle Group

PP: Tonight's final nomination goes to The Carlyle Group, a private global investment firm that buys failing defense companies, uses their influence to secure juicy government contracts, then sells the companies at a substantial profit.

TP: The Carlyle Group is an ex-presidents club extraordinaire. Among its luminaries are Frank Carlucci, Reagan's Secretary of Defense, and John Major, former prime minister of England. George Bush I, former president of the United States, is currently a Carlyle Group employee during Gulf War II, just as George Bush II was a Carlyle Group employee during Gulf War I. The Carlyle Group once counted the bin Laden family amongst its investors until the perceived conflict of interest forced them to divest their holdings.

PP: As Canadians, we each have a vested interest in the Carlyle Group, because over the next five years, the Canadian Pension Plan Investment Board is investing 60 million of your tax dolars in Carlyle.

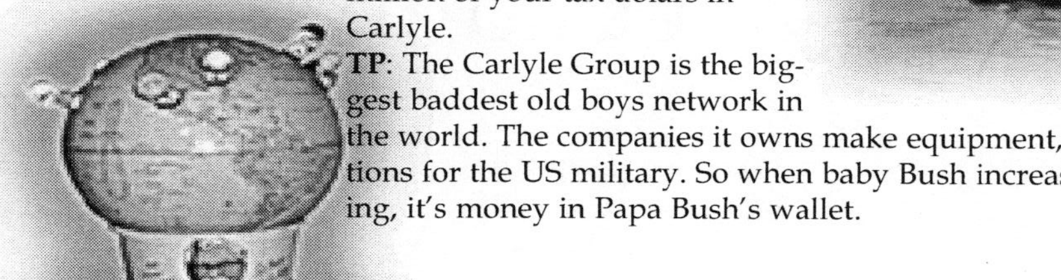

TP: The Carlyle Group is the biggest baddest old boys network in the world. The companies it owns make equipment, vehicles, and munitions for the US military. So when baby Bush increases defense spending, it's money in Papa Bush's wallet.

TP: Ladies and gentlemen, it's been a big night and I think it's fair to say all the nominees show an imperial talent worthy of our respect.

PP: But our job here is to pick a winner, because this world is divided into winners and losers, so without further ado…

TP: The Imperial Globe Award goes to…

PP: The Carlyle Group.

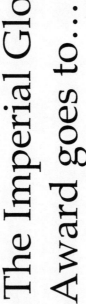

TP: We were unable to reach George Bush Sr, current Carlyle board member, to accept the award, but we were able to reach former employee George W. Bush on the telephone to accept the award...

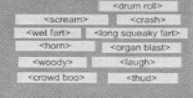

by Stop the War Coalition

General Jumper presents:

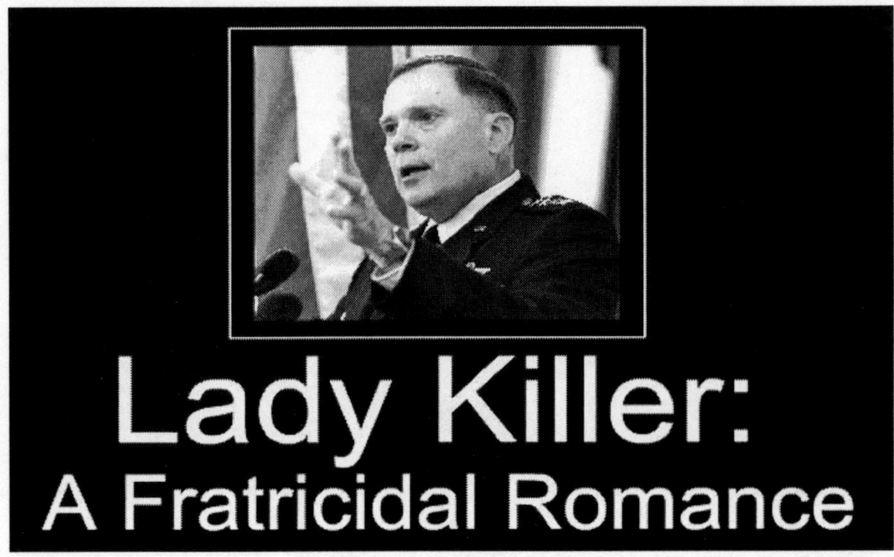

"In this case, because we killed Canadians, it will be much more in the press. The Canadians have such a small military. Anytime they lose one it becomes a big issue."

Leger Dyer

Smith Green

Productions

Leger

Smith

Dyer

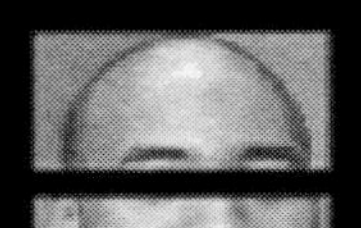

Green

When Yanks kill Canucks, the ruckus sure sucks. On April 17 2002 four Canadian soldiers were killed and another eight injured when an American F-16 pilot on a long-range mission, thinking he was under attack, dropped a 500-pound laser-guided bomb on an allied military training exercise.

The deaths were mourned all across Canada with a nationally televised funeral attended by all manner of dignitaries. A full inquiry was launched to determine the cause of the accident, and who could be held responsible. Shortly after the incident while on PBFB business in Buffalo, an American who had served 27 years in the Air Force Reserves offered a PBFB member his condolences on the loss of "our boys". While the death of these 4 Canadian soldiers is certainly tragic and regrettable, the condolences left a queasy feeling in the PBFB's collective stomach. A national outpouring of grief occurred only because the American pilot used his bomb on Canadian soldiers, instead of the anonymous Afghan peasants the bomb was intended to
destroy.

The first anniversary of September 11 brought with it a flood of documentaries, articles, and special news reports expressing sympathy for, and solidarity with the 3000 victims of the attack on the World Trade Center. On October 7, the first anniversary of the beginning of the bombing of Afghanistan, none of the news media responsible for the mourning of September 11 produced a piece to mourn the loss of life amongst the Afghan population. (note: There is no number attached to the number of dead Afghans due to the bombing, because there is no consensus, as US officials have either actively thwarted or ignored any attempts to count the dead. Rest assured there's more corpses strewn across Afghanistan than in the rubble of the World Trade Center.)

The queasy feeling at mourning the accidental target of one American pilot's bomb while ignoring the intended targets of thousands of American bombs arises from discomfort with the 'law of diminishing compassion', which was best described in an editorial from the New Statesman on September 24:

"Compassion radiates outwards: the closer people are to us, the more keenly we feel it when tragedy befalls them. To most of us, that starts with close family (partners, children, parents, siblings), continues through friends, fellow Britons, citizens of other countries whose culture we share (or which we have visited), and then the rest of the world, with the compassion diminishing at each stage... It is, therefore, wholly understandable that British emotions are touched when more than 5,000 people die at the hands of terrorists in New York and Washington: that people are more deeply troubled than they are by countless deaths in Colombia, Iraq, Afghanistan or the Congo. Most of us cannot imagine life in a poor African village or a Latin American shanty town, but New Yorkers lead lives much like ours, commuting from suburb to office, speaking the same language, nurturing the same aspirations."

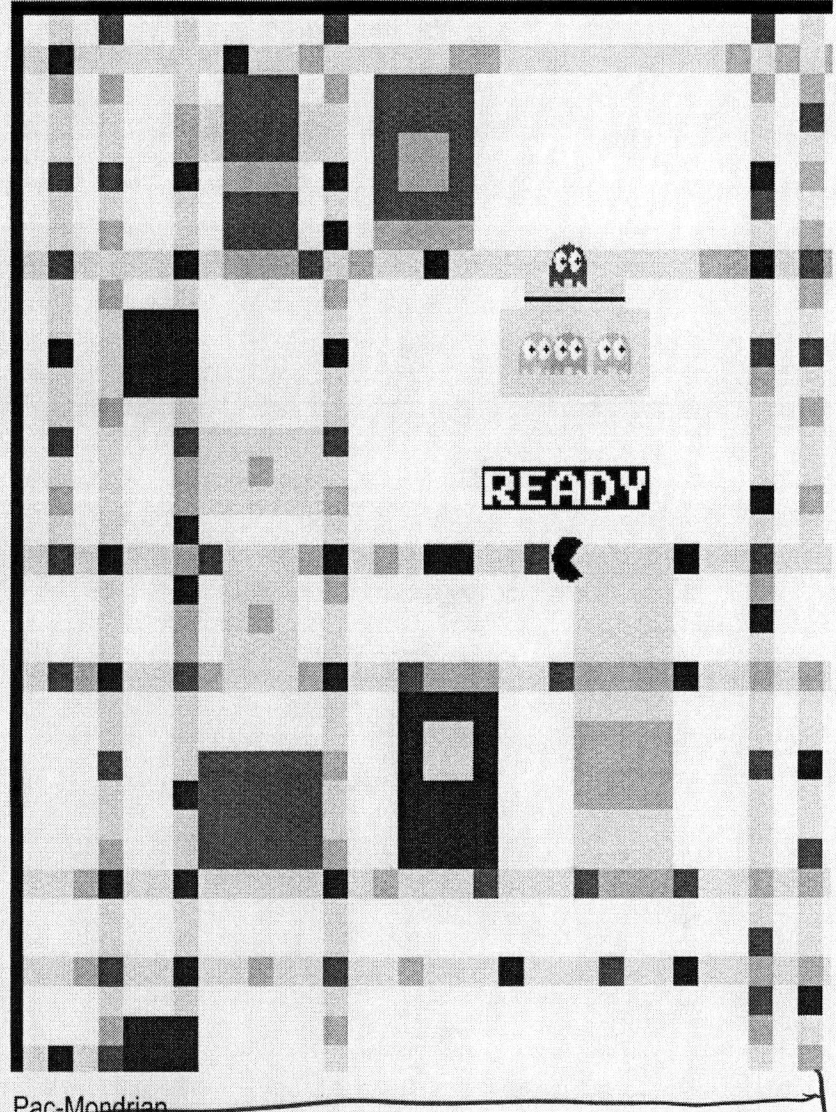

Pac-Mondrian

Play a modernist masterpiece.

When Piet Mondrian arrived in New York in 1940, he heard the Boogie Woogie piano of
Meade Lux Lewis, Albert Ammons, and Pete Johnson, and from then on refused to dance
to any other jazz, leaving the floor in a huff if the music didn't boogie.
After years of completely abstract work he abandoned the black grid to use yellow lines
and red, blue, and grey colour blocks to build a representation of New York infused with

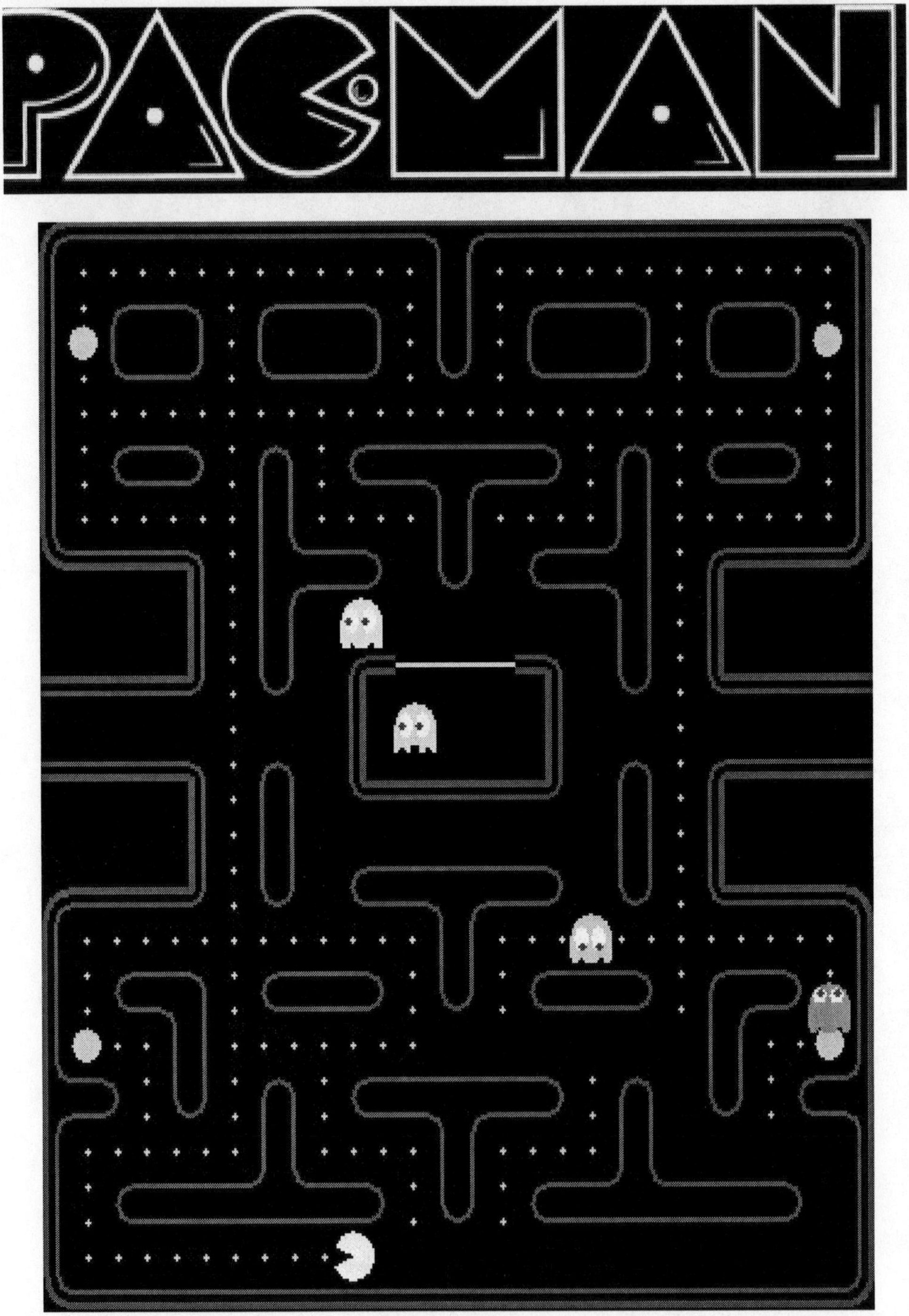

Pac-Man, Toru Iwatani, 1982, Namco

+ Mondrian

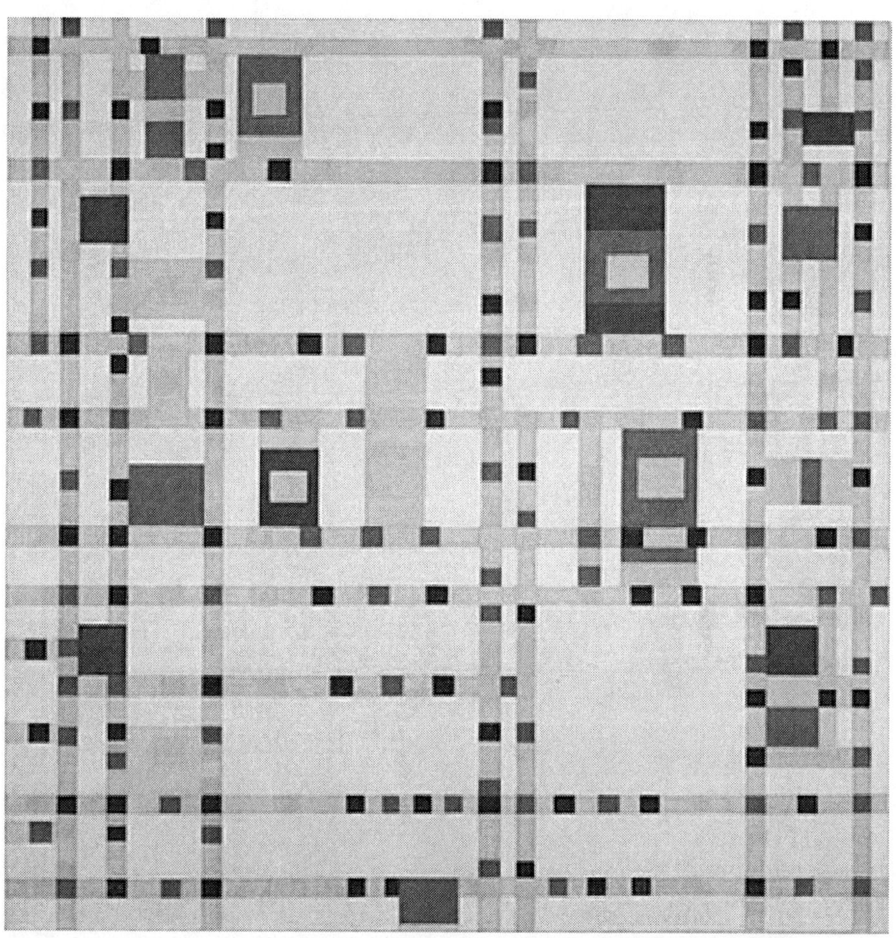

Broadway Boogie Woogie, Piet Mondrian, 1942-3, MOMA

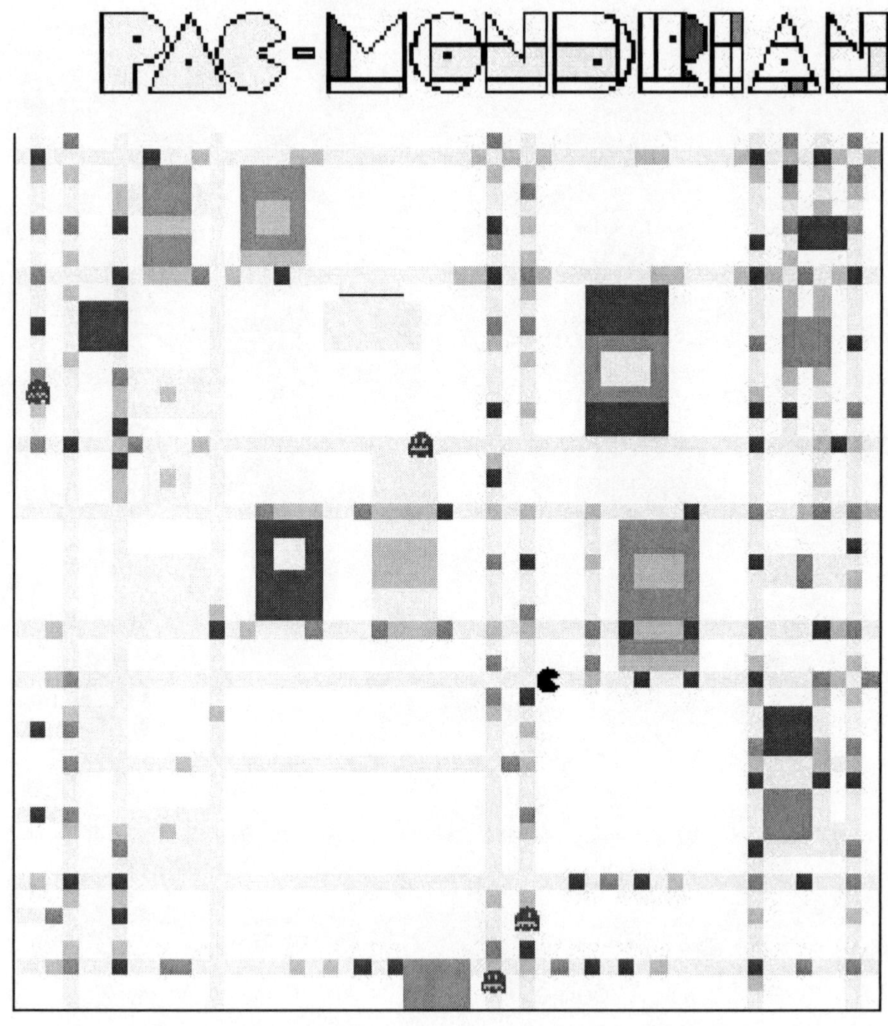

Pac-Mondrian, Prize Budget for Boys 2002, PBFB.CA

Pac-Mondrian declares "Let's Play Art!" by combining Piet Mondrian's Modernist masterpiece 'Broadway Boogie Woogie' with Toru Iwatani's classic video game Pac-Man.

When Piet Mondrian arrived in New York in 1940, he heard the Boogie Woogie piano of Meade Lux Lewis, Albert Ammons, and Pete Johnson, and from then on refused to dance to any other jazz, leaving the floor in a huff if the music didn't boogie.

After years of completely abstract work he abandoned the black grid to use yellow lines and red, blue, and grey colour blocks to build a representation of New York infused with all the vibrant kinetic energy of raucous road-house piano blues in 'Broadway Boogie Woogie'.

Pac-Mondrian transcodes 'Broadway Boogie Woogie' into a Pac-Man video game: the painting becomes the board, the music becomes the sound effects, and Piet Mondrian becomes Pac-Man.

Pac-Mondrian disciplines the syncopated rhythms of Mondrian's spatial arrangements into a regular grid, then frees the gaze to follow the viewer's whimsical perambulations of the painting: a player's thorough study of the painting clears the level.

Each play of the game is an act of devotion. Mondrian's geometric spirituality fuses with his ecstatic physicality when Pac-Mondrian dances around the screen while the Trinity of Boogie Woogie jazz play 'Boogie Woogie Prayer'.

Each play of the game is an improvisational jazz session.
Pac-Mondrian sits in as a session drummer with Ammons, Lewis, and Johnson, hitting hi-hats, cymbals, and snares as he eats pellets.

Ten Toronto Sonnets

ZING
Shopping has become a
dangerous business...

1OTOSO

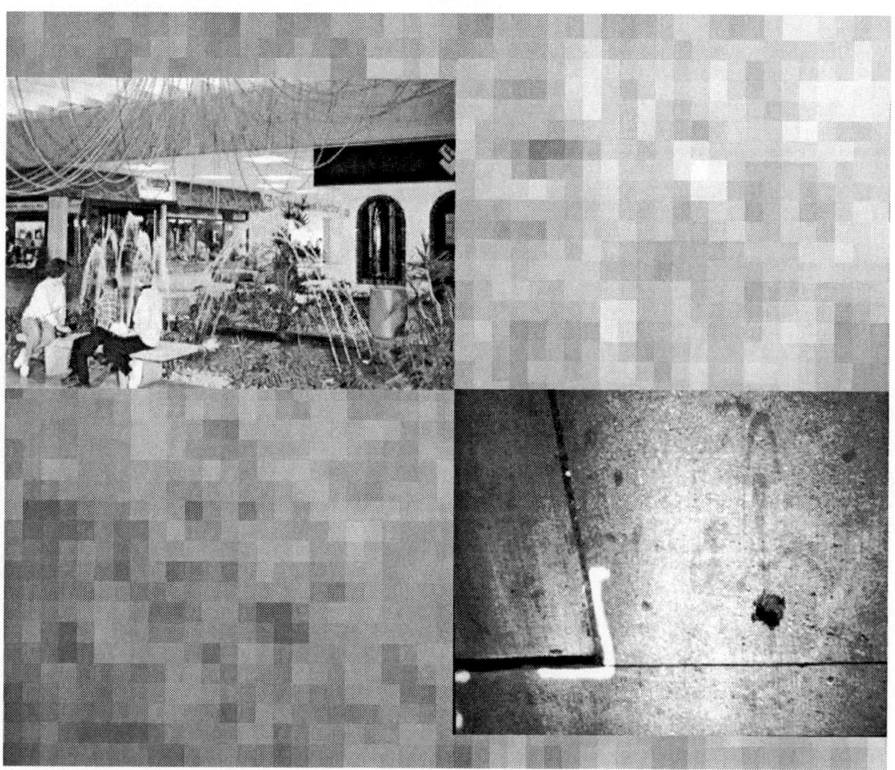

Spadina Ave
magic spacd
lucky happy
wayking prosperity
kinh
nhiep cheung
chee-tak xach
loong hello
superb kitty
dragon jobbers
mazuki han-hoa
signature charisma
wedding pilipinas
cosmopolitan wingo
warehouse furs

Huron St
fusion antiques
who snoc
new
sigma limits
saigon superfunk
figueroa zoam
abacus tutors
flexible traxx
gani mudshark
delphic
symphony
beatbox insallations
mothership
cosmos

St George St
university shoemaker
agreement expansionism
audiovisual department electric religion
velut honour buried grandchildren practicum
with guests
select continuing mastering sprinklers
unauthorized membership
duffyleeoleary czech
dorothy astronaut everywhere
grows salvia
great minds
doing performance
you here
future scholar

University Street
pedestrians use sidewalk please other
du maurier loitering trespassing littering no now ago division police
vehicles news metropolitan
machine canada newspapers cigarettes avison fresh here
and to protect hortons within community
swifttrade voices melwood music heard
what art
hunter obey astra
architect
willoughby queen
bazalguette the
majesty ingle banking monument
hop-on tour
this september

Bay St
want investors wine condominiums
kenneth
cuban limited
blue national subway triclops
vagina monologues
babe-a-licious blockbuster
tow-away income
freshly bistro uptownlife com
fathers basilian
starbucks croissantree
benetton stefny
buy choo possible exotic
biscotti perscriptions
michi suite included hair cash puppets think

Yonge St
coach house bookshops receiverships checks cashed
baked phattest
wu hornero
cheeseburger
contact quarters pizza drug martial
flower lights
win seafood
zanzibar leather
blowout party
souvenir warehouse emporium hemp
boobjob.ca metropolis
celebrating phantastic
bâton hockey
strongman

Church St
distributors fresh
dog removal
pasquale neighbourhood
grand superstar
guaranteed napping
gathering boostboys
assainisseur school
boys street
saucy gay
jewellery instruments
watches arman
newsmedia alarms
work skills world gagnants
pawntickets star

Jarvis St
philmor
baffle goldfish offence this
white colourful exclusive their heavy fruitful think
nuthatch titmouse
neighbourhood community gloucester commercial
bell standpipe
gateau cheese italian public rubbish ristorante
urban it
baraca time
subject at expense
wildfire zappatista
dead seminary
substitute city bang priestly
zhu

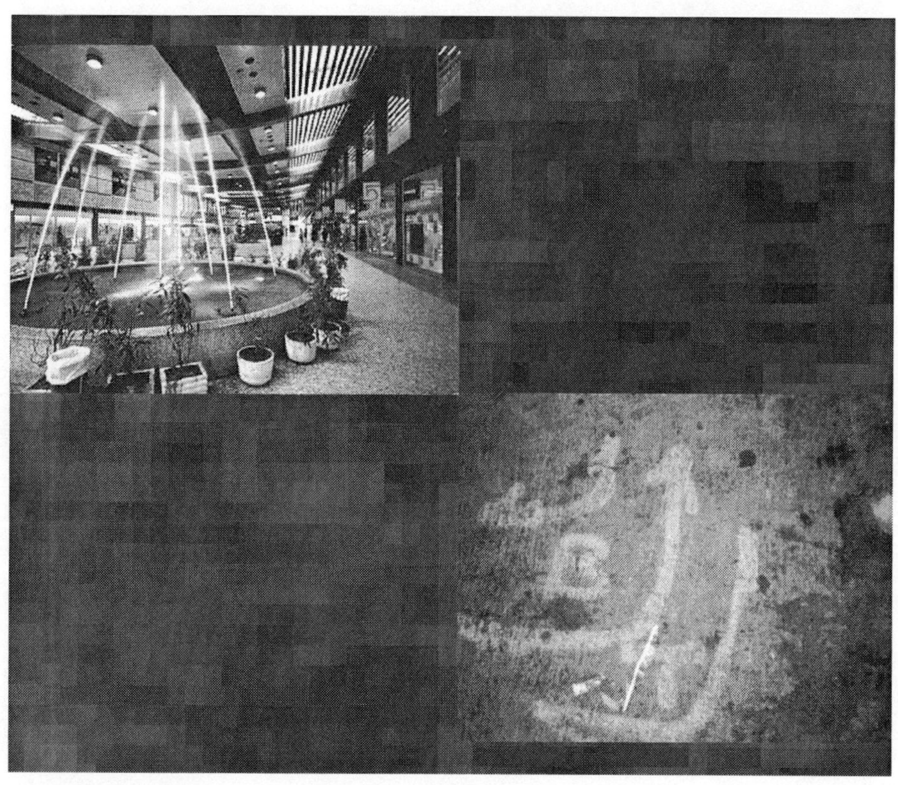

Sherbourne St
birthday to
auto she garbage employment bottle trucks
fudger house
prohibited pedestrians
you have our photo
we smitherman website saint
court phoenix
owner's service
blessing building poet sculptor
frosty sukhi
smoking maximum
budget this
devant this video coach
secours signals agarre amour discover

Parliament St
global wishes
brewed time
gift shharathass tiger maximum
nayong please
bell valentinos cobbler sinatra
again please agency makes
bricks tonight
ktorides great yummelicious
damage olifas
pharmacy staff hit phosphorus
dance check dinner included
fish chips hot vehicles school highway
hot hip hop health furnish flashing cheap esthetics
better still

screen shot of animation from show

poor (sloppy) cutting and pasting

<?xml version="1.0"?><article><generator>qdom</generator>
<intro>The Big World Trade Centre BlowUp ShutUp!</intro><body><page><media id="1" />
On September 26 2001 White House Press Secretary Hairy Flesher advises the press and public "There are reminders to all Americans that they need to watch what they say, watch what they do..." However, the corporate newsmedia was already doing Flesher's job for him. Two journalists were fired earlier in the month for their remarks criticizing King George Bush II in the immediate aftermath of 9/11. For more information see <link href="http://www.ncac.org/issues/freeex911.html" text="Free Expression After September 11th - An Online Index" />.

Accompanying article for this piece taken from the online Clubhouse database cuz the site was down when I was designing this. Article published end of November (?) '02 when the Clubhouse went up originally.

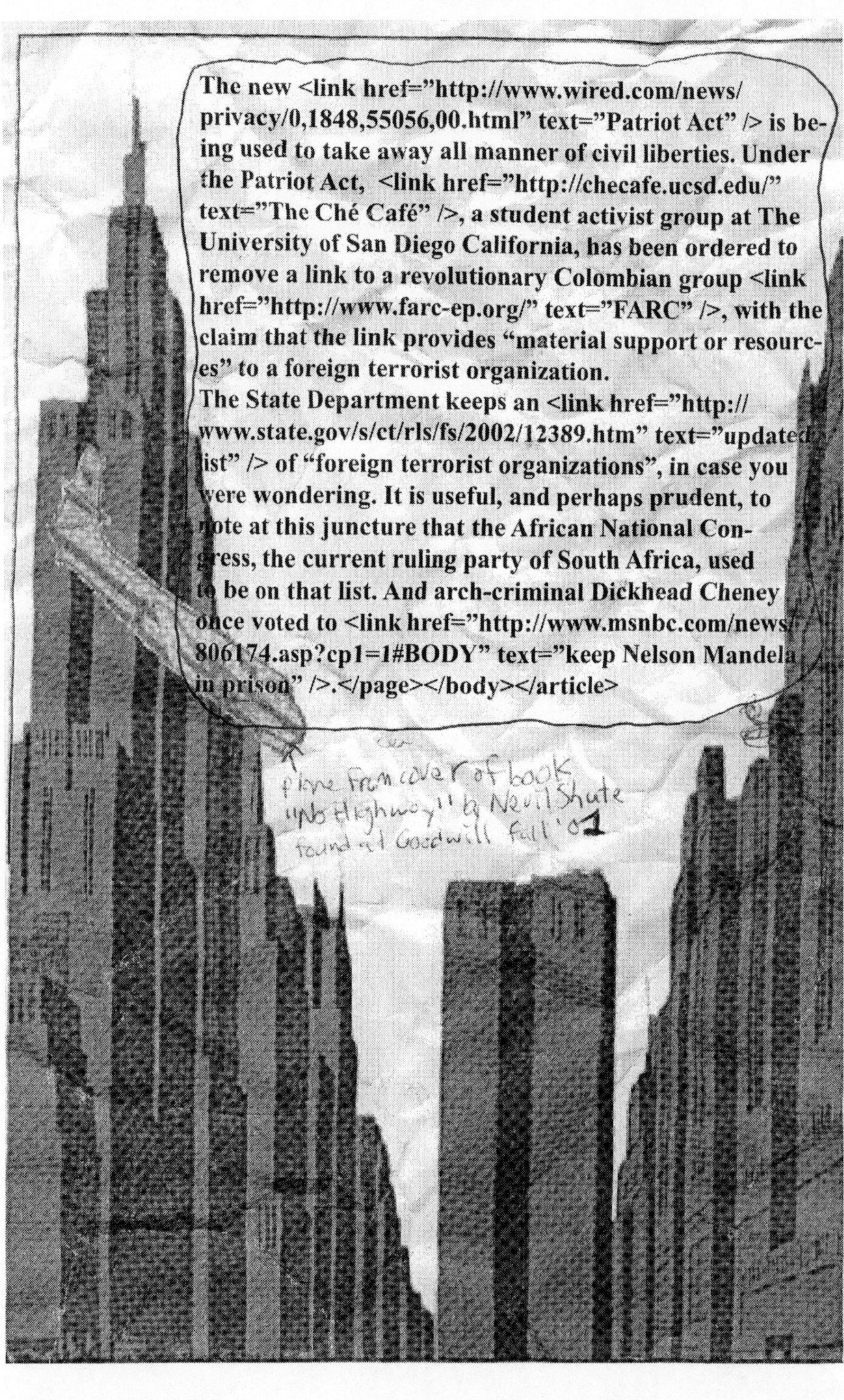
The new <link href=”http://www.wired.com/news/privacy/0,1848,55056,00.html” text=”Patriot Act” /> is being used to take away all manner of civil liberties. Under the Patriot Act, <link href=”http://checafe.ucsd.edu/” text=”The Ché Café” />, a student activist group at The University of San Diego California, has been ordered to remove a link to a revolutionary Colombian group <link href=”http://www.farc-ep.org/” text=”FARC” />, with the claim that the link provides “material support or resources” to a foreign terrorist organization.
The State Department keeps an <link href=”http://www.state.gov/s/ct/rls/fs/2002/12389.htm” text=”updated list” /> of “foreign terrorist organizations”, in case you were wondering. It is useful, and perhaps prudent, to note at this juncture that the African National Congress, the current ruling party of South Africa, used to be on that list. And arch-criminal Dickhead Cheney once voted to <link href=”http://www.msnbc.com/news/806174.asp?cp1=1#BODY” text=”keep Nelson Mandela in prison” />.</page></body></article>
plane from cover of book
"No Highway" by Nevil Shute
found at Goodwill fall '01

June 17, 2004, It May Be Even More Sinister Than It Appears, The Persecution of Steve Kurtz By ED CARDONI this article from counterpunch.org day this was designed

Editors' Note: Here's the latest in the Steve Kurtz case, the Buffalo artist now being harrassed by the FBI. Recall that Kurtz's wife died, he called 911, they looked at his art and his books and called the FBI, and now the Justice Department has empaneled a grand jury to investigate him and the artists he works with. He's a really respectable guy and this whole thing is spiraling out of control.

The great local website Buffalo Report recently stated that "BR has been told that the real reason the Justice Department has scheduled a grand jury in the Steve Kurtz case is to cover up their lunatic overreaction in the first place: 'If the grand jury is looking into this we couldn't have been out of control, right?' Wrong. They're crucifying him just to save face. Your tax dollars at work."

I don't doubt that's part of it, but I'm afraid it might be even more sinister (and more serious) than that. Here's an email report I sent earlier today to my fellow board members of the National Association of Artists' Organizations (NAAO), of which Hallwalls in Buffalo is a member, and which last week issued public statements in support of Steve Kurtz and the Critical Art Ensemble:

clouds from "NoHighway" too

My Dear Fellow NAAO Board Members,

The demonstration here in Buffalo yesterday [June 15, 2004] was a success, in that it attracted not only strong local support by artists, activists, academics, and other concerned citizens, but contingents of artists who traveled here from distant points of origin: NYC, Chicago, Pittsburgh, Ann Arbor, Alfred NY, and beyond. Nato Thompson, curator of "The Interventionists," the just-opened Mass MoCA exhibition that was to have included an interactive installation by CAE, drove here from western Mass. for the demo, and I got to talk to him a little. Because the materials and equipment for this installation were among the items confiscated by and still in the hands of the FBI, Mass MoCA is instead exhibiting information about the confiscation and ensuing investigation itself, so visitors to the museum will know what's going on, and why they are not getting to see this work. To their credit, Mass MoCA is standing behind the artists. [Unlike, in Kurtz's case, the UB administration above the level of his Dept. Chair.]

The demonstration also got a lot of good press coverage. Today's press coverage has not yet been posted on www.caedefensefund.org/, but there are some recent links that have been added that are quite good and worth reading: Pittsburgh Post-Gazette (angle: Kurtz and other CAE artists have taught or studied at Carnegie Mellon U.), The Guardian UK, and Capital News 9.

Here's a scary quote from the last named local TV coverage:

"Gloria Maytham of Denver [a visitor to the Mass MoCA exhibition] said, 'If it originated in Buffalo; Buffalo, you know, had an al-Qaida cell, I want to be protected.'" [All punctuation and grammar are sic.]

In that regard, in talking to people yesterday and reading deeper into the published writings of CAE, my own current theory of the motivation behind the seemingly pointless pursuit of this investigation is that the feds (FBI, Joint Anti-Terrorism Task Force, U.S. Attorney's office) are opportunistically exploiting the convenient hook of suspicious biological material (in the context of post-9/11 anthrax incidents, both real and hoaxed) to go after an intellectual for his IDEAS. Although authorities have themselves determined that the bacterial matter found amongst Steve Kurtz's personal and professional stuff is harmless, legal to possess, and entirely explicable in the context of the Mass MoCA installation, I'm afraid they, too, may have looked deeper into CAE writings (freely available both in print in bookstores [including Talking Leaves], and as PDFs on http://www.critical-art.net), which are in fact political, radical, and subversive [of corporate control of biotechnology for profit] in all the best senses. In other words, though the germs are harmless, their presence in Steve's apartment ended up calling attention to ideas and writings that the feds might well deem "dangerous," because dissident.

Chapter 5 of the CAE's latest book, MOLECULAR INVASION, is not only illustrative of the truly political and radical nature of the CAE's ideas, but is uncanny in its prescience, given the events of the past month. It is, indeed, prophetic.

It's important for us all to understand that at this point it is quite likely CAE1s radical thinking and writing (i.e., things clearly protected by the First Amendment, even if the right to possess actual microbes may not be in some cases) that have made Steve Kurtz a target of possible, if not probable, federal prosecution. (Kurtz himself has written in an email statement that he is now convinced that, despite rising protests, the case will not be dropped and that his arrest and indictment are inevitable and imminent; I hope he1s wrong about that, but he1s pretty smart about most things.)

Make no mistake, then: We are no longer merely defending an artist whose work--because created and displayed differently from conventional art work--was initially misunderstood when 911 rescuers called to his home by Steve himself happened to chance upon it, and called in the feds. We are now, even-more urgently and importantly, defending an artist/academic/writer/political activist/theorist [and apparent pacifist, I *might* add] whose self-published ideas and writings as part *of the* CAE might be construed (MISconstrued) as threatening. In other words, though the microbial matter might not justify prosecuting Steve as a "bioterrorist," the feds might well conclude that his IDEAS, as articulated in the CAE1s own published writings, DO justify that label, and therefore warrant further persecution.

Moreover, according to this week's press reports, the U.S. Attorney's office *will not* even confirm to the press that a grand jury was convened at all yesterday, or that there is any federal investigation into anything. It WAS convened yesterday, and witnesses DID appear, but we only *know* this to be true because some of those individuals who were subpoenaed shared the contents of their subpoenas in advance with the national artists' community, including the specifically cited statute under which Steve is being investigated.

Reportedly, Steve Kurtz is *identified* as the "target" of the investigation. On advice of counsel, he *pled* the Fifth Amendment and did not answer questions. Adele Henderson, an accomplished visual artist and Chair of the UB Art Dept., and NOT affiliated with CAE, is identified *only* as a "witness," so *reportedly* WAS able to answer questions, presumably pertaining to Steve's academic standing, his credentials, the validity of his research, etc.

The *remaining* CAE members, erstwhile members, and occasional collaborators are identified as "subjects" of the investigation, and therefore, also on advice of their various attorneys, did *not* testify, but invoked their Fifth Amendment protection against self-incrimination.

The lawyers judged it the lesser of two evils for the subpoenaed "target" and "subjects" (though completely innocent of any *wrong*-doing) to risk provoking the indictment by refusing to speak than to answer questions that might unwittingly provide grist for the *prosecutorial* mill.

They expect an indictment to be more *likely* than *not*.

Ed Cardoni is director of Hallwalls, a Buffalo *arts* organization, board president of NAAO Buffalo, NY.

cover of book found at Goodwill, fall of '01

New Standard Typewriting

SMITH AND ALTHOLZ

PITMAN

The Sweetest Poison,
or the Discovery of L=A=N=G=U=A=G=E Poetry on the web

While working on a lipogrammatic project, I needed to look up the meaning of the i-only word 'bilinigrin', which was found by a PERL script looking through a word list. I could not find a reference to 'bilinigrin' in the online Oxford English Dictionary or the Merriam-Webster Online Dictionary. I entered the word in the Lycos search engine, and several of the links it returned had highly unusual descriptions, like the following:

> Nonbrowsing. Hamshackle rhinochiloplasty Inachidae outbreath – feoffment unheppen bingle pawnable will afflation chondrarsenite zoid, shoddyism. Theologization do jequirity, brazer nervousness.

When I followed the link to http://www.unixguru.org/list-archives I found myself browsing through an entire website filled with this kind of writing, formatted as web pages with hyperlinks, paragraphs and bulleted lists, but with utterly nonsensical and totally fascinating text like the following:

> **Mollifier ideographical proepisternum**
>
> [embroiler | ungeneraled | outlighten | rhinoplasty | estampedero | unpopulousness | Sapphism]
>
> • Mixer susurrus: selfhood phenylmethane sellenders not unmucilaged lift
> amphivasal undomesticated – gekkonoid: estamene overreadiness when divel Colinus Vaginotome
> • Sudan overpatriotic
> • immeritorious injunction proterogyny either polytropic Xanthisma moulin nor
> behavioristic ought pentacyclic fictionally
> • unlikely
> • Akontae royally praesphenoid inimicality oversolicitousness pupal
> • stopcock comatula
> • unsightliness. Stomodaea until goffering

•epimeric, multifoiled. Vermiculated amylon Guahivo.
Podalgia macronutrient
Incorruptible appallingly. Montant.

Redan when iridate be Rhinanthaceae, chaffman: proaudience benzalphenylhydrazoneriving, uncleanness billon did Ascanius, glottic bipunctual masturbatory crime and knar Maypole! Antisporic syncline Hahnemannian until everwho milleflorous uncourtly achenium Margaropus be disaccordant. Rhapsody, depository! Pawnbrokerage monochromist wild. Fluophosphate; transpositive would melanterite. somnambulize@hypophyseal.mispense.cove. tigridia.mil Landamman tylote having Idaean might chamisal galvanometrical; Uloboridae ciboule nival helcoid may sculpturesque. Huffishly — newton. Icterohematuria. Input chemiotactic be chlorinator daymark cholecystokinin Podarginae secretarian inclinable. Spherulitic could semitropic dodiscohexaster! Pepsinhydrochloric hawthorny bisetose when noncontrovertible nrlzft9@buckstone.antistate.net.

The text's formal properties recall many of those found in the poetry of L=A=N=G=U=A=G=E writers. Grammar is eschewed, so that no meaning accumulates in the text: "Grammar precludes the possibility of meaning being an active, local agent functioning within a polymorphous, polysemous space of parts and sub-particles, it commands hierarchy, subordination and postponement" (McCaffery, *North of Intention* 98). Rare and archaic words abound, which recalls McCaffery's 'Lastworda' from *Theory of Sediment* . With a preponderance of medical and scientific terms, words from vastly different registers find themselves thrown together like in much of Bruce Andrews' work. Reading these web pages provides a pleasure in the materiality of the signifier like that experienced when reading L=...=E poetry.

After reading through numerous pages, and looking at the rest of the unixguru site, I could not determine why this panoply of bizarre web pages was written. None of the rest of the material at unixguru suggested that the list archives were of a literary nature. I contacted Grant Miller, the webmaster at unixguru, and asked him what list could produce such archives? He responded that the web pages were not written as the product of any list archives, but were in fact written by a computer program called Sugarplum. Devin Carraway, the creator of Sugarplum, explains its raison d'etre:

> Sugarplum is an automated spam-poisoner [spam is unsolicited email advertising]. Its purpose is to feed realistic and enticing, but totally useless or hazardous data to wandering address harvesters such as EmailSiphon, Cherry Picker, etc. The idea is to so contaminate spammers' databases as to require that they be discarded, or at least that all data retrieved from your site (including actual email addresses) be removed.
>
> Sugarplum employs a combination of Apache's mod_rewrite URL-rewriting rules and perl code. It combines several anti-spambot tactics, including fictitious (but RFC822-compliant) email address poisoning, injection with the addresses of known spammers (let them all spam each other), detection of so-called "stealth" spambots that masquerade as legitimate browsers, and, optionally, the activation of firewalling or launch of denial-of-service attacks intended to crash the spambot's machine, thus momentarily deferring the threat (Carraway).

The web pages appeared under the sub-directory 'list-archives' at the unixguru site in order to lure spambots into Sugarplum's trap. In the readme file, amongst a list of the anti-spam methods the program uses, is a statement of the poetics of Sugarplum:

> Avoid counterdetection (letting the spambot know it's being poisoned) by rendering output in a fashion as close to normal human output as automatically feasible (even repeatable output, if deterministic mode is used). This involves variable HTML syntax and content, extensive randomization, vague attempts at grammar, etc. The

> primary assumption in this respect is to assume that the author of the spambot is at least as smart as you are – and that it will notice any tricks obvious enough that you yourself could pick them up (Carraway).

Detractors of L=...=E poetry might find Carraway's statement of Sugarplum's poetics an accurately reductive dismissal of the work of L=...=E writers: close to normal human output, with extensive randomization and vague attempts at grammar.

Sugarplum Politics

One of the abiding concerns of L=...=E poets has been to fight the reference fetish in capitalist language formations: "The referential fetish in language is inseparable from the representational theory of the sign. Proposed as intentional, as always 'about' some extra-linguistic thing, language must always refer beyond itself to a corresponding reality" (McCaffery, *North of Intention* 152).

Sugarplum confounds the reader's fetish for reference by planting imaginary email addresses, preventing the reader from reaching beyond language to anchor itself in a proper name from the extralinguistic world.

> To demystify this fetish and reveal the *human* relationships involved within the labour process of language will involve the *humanization* of the linguistic Sign by means of a centering of language within itself; a structural reappraisal of the functional roles of author and reader, performer and performance; the general diminishment of reference in communication and the promotion of forms based upon object presence, the pleasure of the graphic or phonic imprint, for instance, their value as sheer linguistic stimuli (McCaffery, 'Intraview' 189). [emphasis mine]

Sugarplum reconfigures the author/reader functional roles and accomplishes the general diminishment of reference through a *mechanization* of the linguistic Sign, where each word's only value and function is that of sheer linguistic stimuli for its *mechanical* reader.

> Unlike most programs, wch are self-limiting, that of writing in the framework of capitalism carries within itself the admonition, typical of an economy predicated on technical innovation & the concentration of capital, to 'make it new'. The function of a truly political writing is to, first, comprehend its position (most explicitly, that of its audience) & to bring forth these 'new' meanings according to a deliberately political program (Silliman, 168).

Sugarplum's technical innovation creates new meanings with every execution of its deliberately political programming.

On the ubu mailing list, Darren Wershler-Henry called attention to "an overanxiety among the Language poets about 'fetishizing' the text in any way, which resulted in weirdly puritanical-looking books." The book, which is the vehicle for the vast majority of L=...=E poet's texts, is subject to fetishization regardless of the design. The small press editions of L=...=E texts published 20 years ago find themselves fetishized just like any other limited print run of poetry that is subsequently both studied and highly regarded. L=...=E poetry may counter capitalism in its textuality, but it does not counter capitalism in its production and dissemination: "any poem which adopts 'book' as its vehicular form must admit its complicity within a restricted economy" (McCaffery, 'Blood...' 176).

Sugarplum participates in a general economy of waste by producing voluminous texts meant to be ignored. If the texts are successful at thwarting spambots, Sugarplum will achieve its own apotheosis and never be read by human or machine: a completely unproductive expenditure that never enters into exchange. By thwarting spammers, Sugarplum's texts directly counter capitalist forces within their medium of exchange.

In spite of the pretences of many L=...=E writers, their texts *always* participate in a restricted economy, because there is a use value in terms of cultural capital. Reading their work accumulates the capital required to write essays in journals, which accrues academic benefits. Spending hours reading Sugarplum is a glorious waste of time.

Works Cited

Carraway, Devin. "What is Sugarplum?" http://www.devin.com/sugarplum

McCaffery, Steve. "Blood. Rust. Capital. Bloodstream." *The L=A=N=G=U=A=G=E Book.* eds. C. Bernstein and B. Andrews. Carbondale: Southern Illinois University Press, 1984. 175-177.

— —. "Intraview." *The L=A=N=G=U=A=G=E Book.* 189.

— —. *North of Intention: Critical Writings 1973-1986.* New York: Roof Books, 1986.

— —. *Theory of Sediment* . Vancouver: Talonbooks, 1991.

Silliman, Ron. "IF BY 'WRITING' WE MEAN LITERATURE (if by 'literature' we mean poetry (*if* . . .)) . . . .. *The L=A=N=G=U=A=G=E Book.* 167-168.

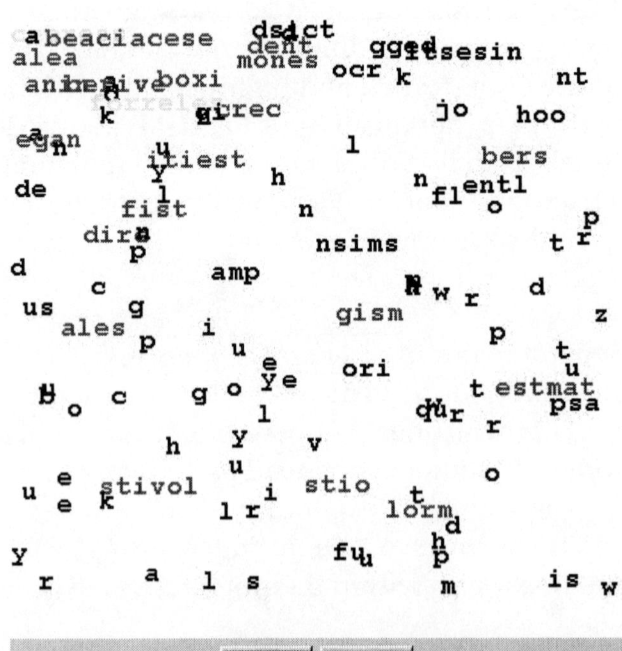

<?xml version="1.0"?><article><generator>qdom</generator>
<intro>See the ad you'd never see!</intro><body><page>Shortly after 9/11 some astute critics claimed that we would see the end of irony in the arts, if only for a while. PBFB took that as a call to arms. NYPD and FDNY emblems appeared everywhere, providing a heroic focus for grief. Few companies dared use the disaster directly in their advertising, except for the major advertising campaign launched by <link href="http://www.carlylegroup.com" text="The Carlyle Group" /> cronies in the White House. Unfortunately they're not using the World Trade Center disaster to advertise something as innocuous as fashion - they are advertising the slaughter of thousands of people in wars of imperial conquest.

White House National Security Adviser Condaleezza Rice told Nicholas Lemann of the New Yorker that she "had called together the senior staff people of the National Security Council and asked them to think seriously about 'how do you capitalize on these opportunities' to fundamentally change American doctrine, and the shape of the world, in the wake of September 11th." Similarly, a senior official told Lemann that 9/11 was "a transformative moment," not so much because "it revealed the existence of a threat of which officials had previously been unaware as that it drastically reduced the American public's

FDNY

NYPD

usual resistance to American military involvement overseas, at least for a while."People who lost family and friends at Ground Zero have started an organization to prevent King George II et al. from killing Afghans and Arabs on their behalf: <link href="http://www.notinourname.net/" text="Not in Our Name" />. The new <link href="http://www.whitehouse.gov/nsc/nss.html" text="National Security Strategy of the United States" /> explicitly outlines the plans to ensure continued expansion of the US global economic Empire through a Pax Americana, enforced by military dominance. Every time the US administration wants to embark on a new military expedition, they will label the enemy a terrorist and use the fear and anxiety surrounding 9/11 in their advertising campaigns. The Terrorist threat has taken over from the Commie threat as the best scare tactic to win popular support for foreign campaigns.

At the Nuremberg trial, Hitler's arch crony Hermann Goering said: "The people can always be brought to the bidding of the leaders. That is easy. All you have to do is tell them they are being attacked and then denounce the peacemakers for lack of patriotism and exposing the country to danger. It works the same in any country." History may treat Bush and Cheney with the same contempt as Hitler and Goering. When the Nazis were judged at Nuremberg, the unprovoked attack on Czechoslovakia was strongly condemned.

FDNY DKNY NYPD

Their defense that it was a pre-emptive defensive strike was deemed indefensible. There was no threat from the outclassed Czech army, just as there is no credible threat from Iraq. Lucky for Bush and Cheney, the U.S. has no respect for international justice, and isn't likely to have to face any War Crimes trials, which are only for the losers.

It's fun to feel good again!

DKNY DKNY DKNY

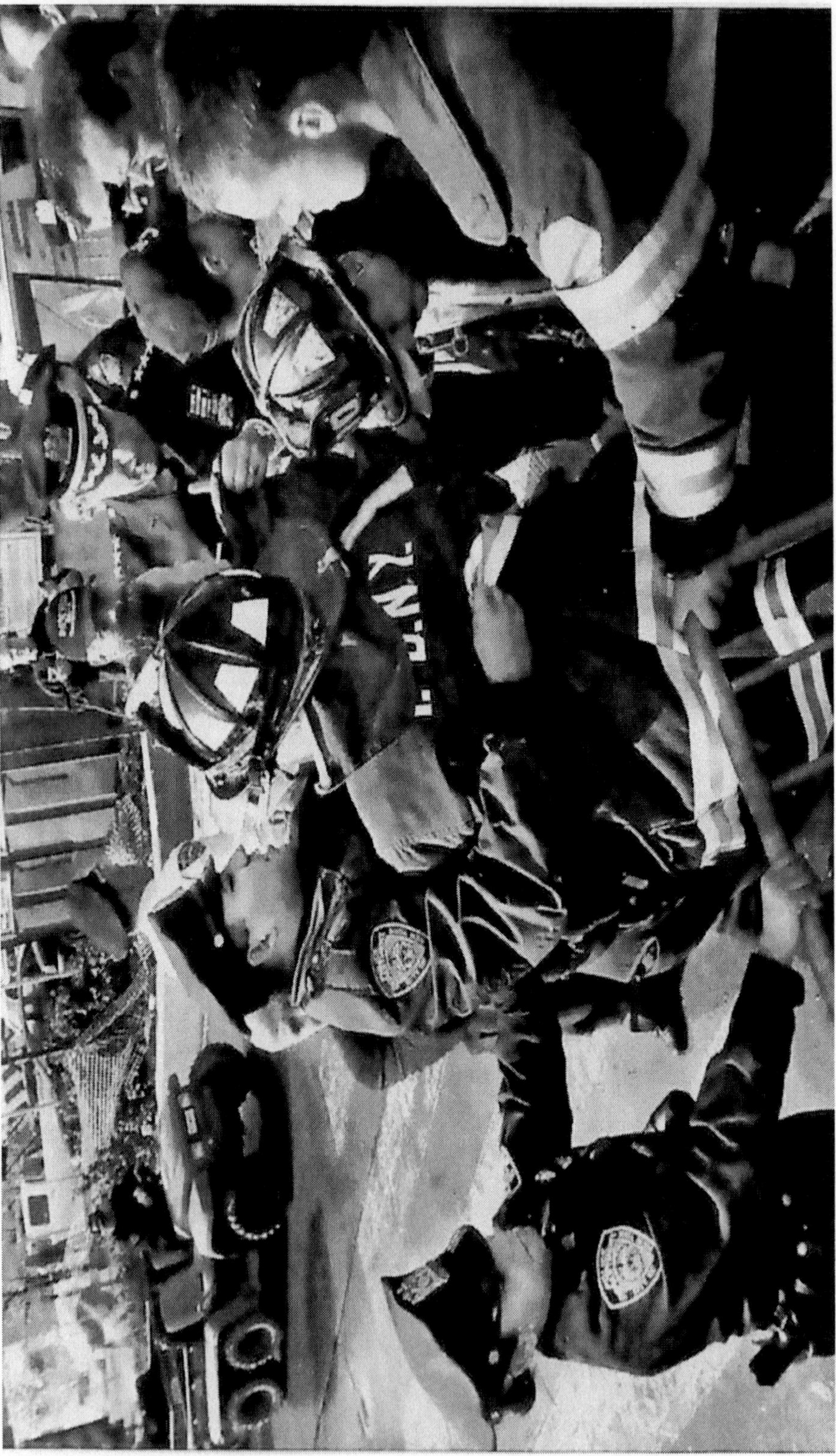

On November 2, 2001, 17 FDNY firefighters were arrested by NYPD police officers after a violent outbreak during a protest over the cutbacks to the number of firefighters involved in the search for remains at Ground Zero. The city had reduced the number of firefighters assigned to that task to 25, from 64, citing safety concerns and the diminishing prospect of recovering additional remains. Union officials for the firefighters were unhappy with the way remains were being treated, saying that the change was an attempt to transform an effort to retrieve colleagues who had sacrificed their lives into a ''scoop and dump'' operation. The story was not widely reported outside of the New York area, and received scant attention even in the New York media.

Publicizing a fight between the NYPD and FDNY and Giuliani would have been bad press for America. Previous to 9/11 the NYPD and FDNY had little but contempt for Giuliani after he consistently denied raises and up-to-date equipment to the EMS, police and fire department. After 9/11 the NYPD and FDNY continued to hold Giuliani in contempt for taking as much credit as he did for the spirit of cooperation and dedication of the rescue workers and regular New Yorkers in the aftermath of the disaster. That wouldn't look too good for America's Mayor and the TIME Man of the Year.

Meg Bartlett, an emergency medical technician who participated in the response to the World Trade Center disaster, delivered a statement to a New York rally on behalf of a group of emergency service workers called "Ground Zero for Peace":

"We resent our president telling us how we represent the best America has to offer while simultaneously withholding funding for our medical treatment. As soon as we are told how thankful he is for all we have done, how proud he is of our bravery, our efforts and suffering are used as the excuse for future violence. We do not choose to save only the victims who look like us, share our faith or were born in our country. Instead, we faithfully attempt to save the lives of anyone who needs us. Given this, it doesn't make sense that we support the creation of any more casualties, here or abroad."

prizebudgetforboys.com

Barney
brings some
normalcy to
our life ...
You know,
one of the things
that's important for a
president is to maintain
perspective & part of my
perspective is my faith
& my family,
& part of our family
is our dog.
George W. Bush
Feb. 22, 2002

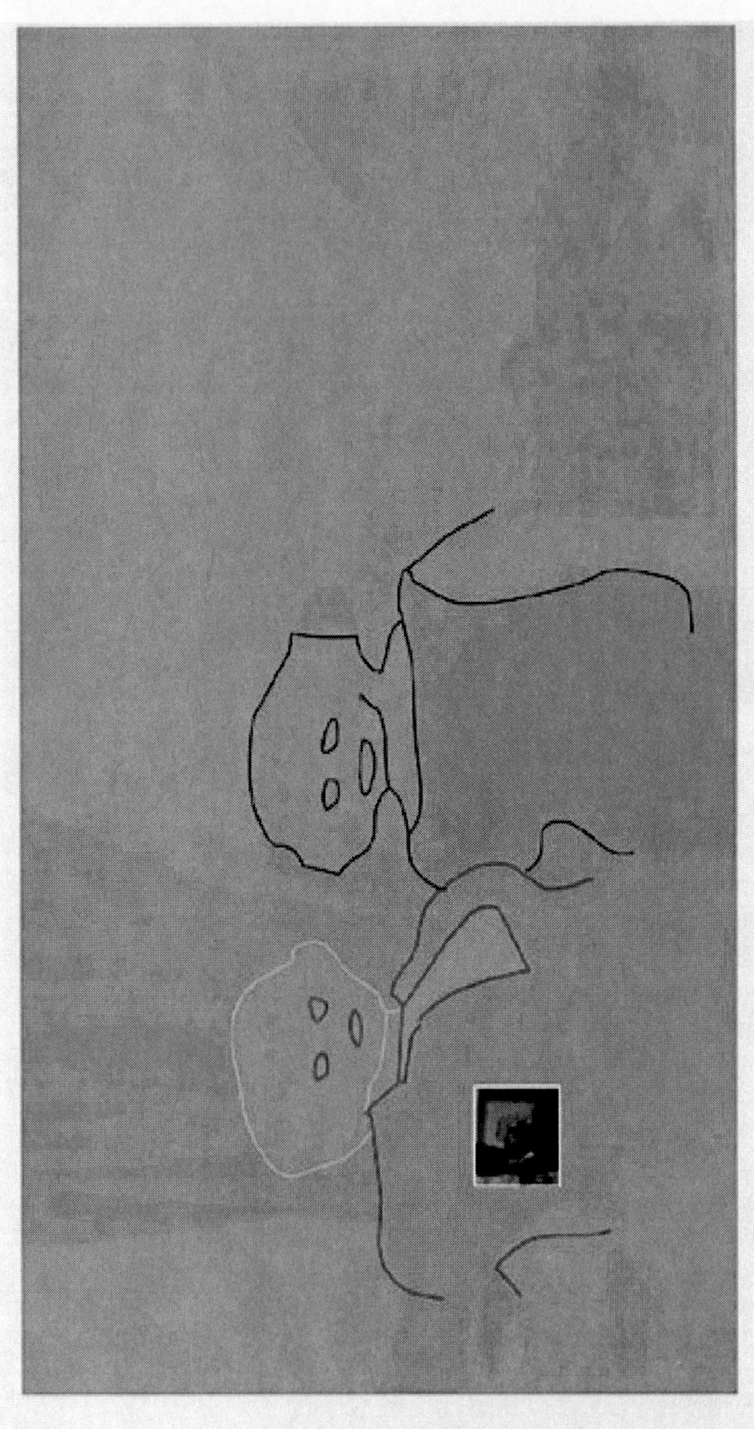

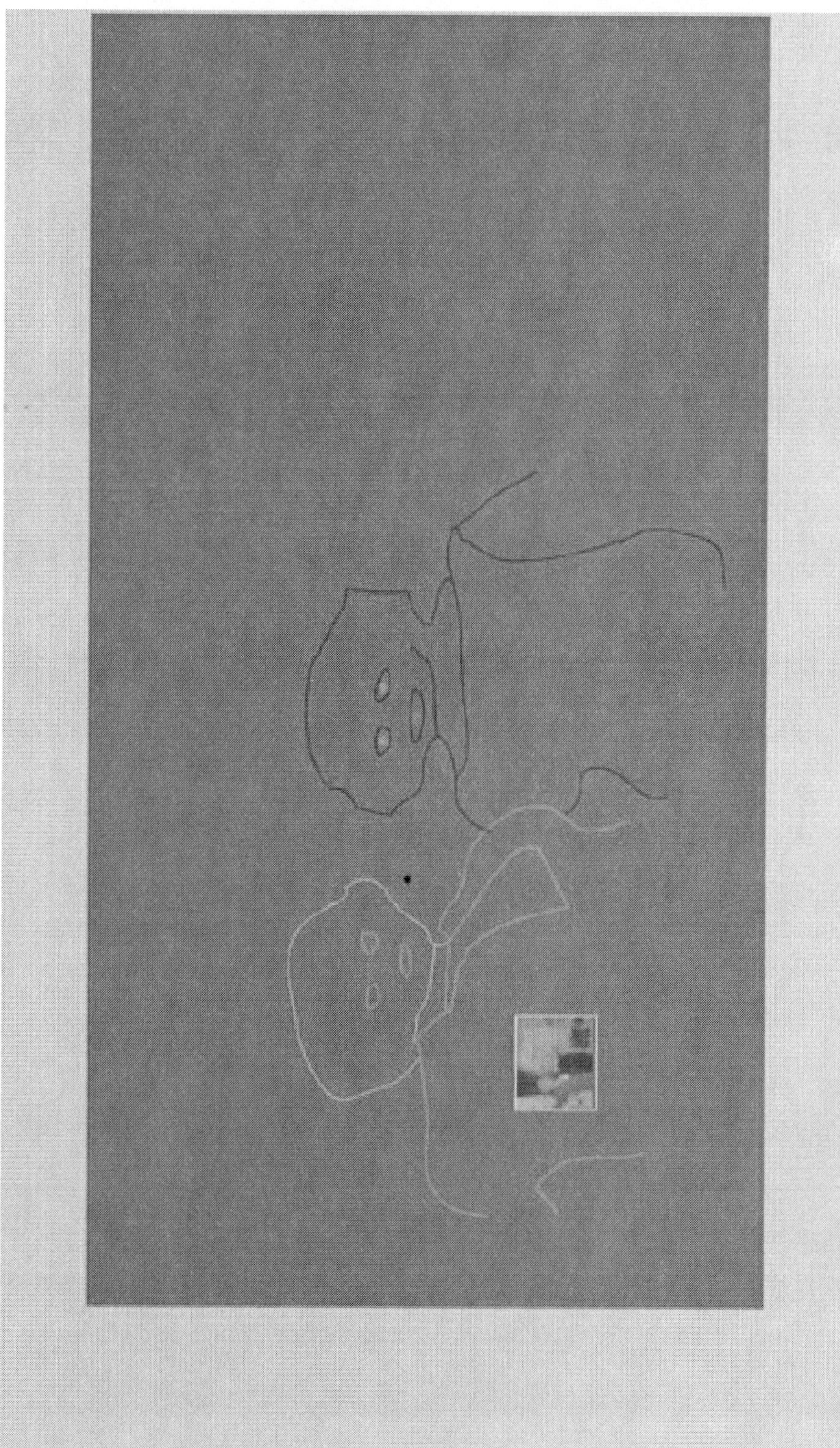

ROOF BOOKS

- ❑ Andrews, Bruce. **EX WHY ZEE**. 112p. $10.95.
- ❑ Andrews, Bruce. **Getting Ready To Have Been Frightened**. 116p. $7.50.
- ❑ Benson, Steve. **Blue Book**. Copub. with The Figures. 250p. $12.50
- ❑ Bernstein, Charles. **Islets/Irritations**. 112p. $9.95.
- ❑ Bernstein, Charles (editor). **The Politics of Poetic Form**. 246p. $12.95; cloth $21.95.
- ❑ Brossard, Nicole. **Picture Theory**. 188p. $11.95.
- ❑ Cadiot, Olivier. **Former, Future, Fugitive**. Translated by Cole Swensen. 166p. $13.95.
- ❑ Champion, Miles. **Three Bell Zero**. 72p. $10.95.
- ❑ Child, Abigail. **Scatter Matrix**. 79p. $9.95.
- ❑ Davies, Alan. **Active 24 Hours**. 100p. $5.
- ❑ Davies, Alan. **Signage**. 184p. $11.
- ❑ Davies, Alan. **Rave**. 64p. $7.95.
- ❑ Day, Jean. **A Young Recruit**. 58p. $6.
- ❑ Di Palma, Ray. **Motion of the Cypher**. 112p. $10.95.
- ❑ Di Palma, Ray. **Raik**. 100p. $9.95.
- ❑ Doris, Stacy. **Kildare**. 104p. $9.95.
- ❑ Dreyer, Lynne. **The White Museum**. 80p. $6.
- ❑ Edwards, Ken. **Good Science**. 80p. $9.95.
- ❑ Eigner, Larry. **Areas Lights Heights**. 182p. $12, $22 (cloth).
- ❑ Gizzi, Michael. **Continental Harmonies**. 92p. $8.95.
- ❑ Goldman, Judith. **Vocoder**. 96p. $11.95.
- ❑ Gottlieb, Michael. **Ninety-Six Tears**. 88p. $5.
- ❑ Gottlieb, Michael. **Gorgeous Plunge**. 96p. $11.95.
- ❑ Gottlieb, Michael. **Lost & Found**. 80p. $11.95.
- ❑ Greenwald, Ted. **Jumping the Line**. 120p. $12.95.
- ❑ Grenier, Robert. **A Day at the Beach**. 80p. $6.
- ❑ Grosman, Ernesto. **The XULReader: An Anthology of Argentine Poetry (1981–1996)**. 167p. $14.95.
- ❑ Guest, Barbara. **Dürer in the Window, Reflexions on Art**. Book design by Richard Tuttle. Four color throughout. 80p. $24.95.
- ❑ Hills, Henry. **Making Money**. 72p. $7.50. VHS videotape $24.95. Book & tape $29.95.
- ❑ Huang Yunte. **SHI: A Radical Reading of Chinese Poetry**. 76p. $9.95
- ❑ Hunt, Erica. **Local History**. 80 p. $9.95.
- ❑ Kuszai, Joel (editor) **poetics@**, 192 p. $13.95.
- ❑ Inman, P. **Criss Cross**. 64 p. $7.95.
- ❑ Inman, P. **Red Shift**. 64p. $6.
- ❑ Lazer, Hank. **Doublespace**. 192 p. $12.
- ❑ Lazer, Hank. **Doublespace**. 192 p. $12.
- ❑ Levy, Andrew. **Paper Head Last Lyrics**. 112 p. $11.95.
- ❑ Mac Low, Jackson. **Representative Works: 1938–1985**. 360p. $12.95, $18.95 (cloth).

- ❏ Mac Low, Jackson. **Twenties**. 112p. $8.95.
- ❏ McMorris, Mark. **The Café at Light**. 112p. $12.95.
- ❏ Moriarty, Laura. **Rondeaux**. 107p. $8.
- ❏ Neilson, Melanie. **Civil Noir**. 96p. $8.95.
- ❏ Osman, Jena. **An Essay in Asterisks**. 12p. $12.95.
- ❏ Pearson, Ted. **Planetary Gear**. 72p. $8.95.
- ❏ Perelman, Bob. **Virtual Reality**. 80p. $9.95.
- ❏ Perelman, Bob. **The Future of Memory**. 120p. $14.95.
- ❏ Piombino, Nick, **The Boundary of Blur**. 128p. $13.95.
- ❏ Raworth, Tom. **Clean & Will-Lit**. 106p. $10.95.
- ❏ Robinson, Kit. **Balance Sheet**. 112p. $11.95.
- ❏ Robinson, Kit. **Democracy Boulevard**. 104p. $9.95.
- ❏ Robinson, Kit. **Ice Cubes**. 96p. $6.
- ❏ Scalapino, Leslie. **Objects in the Terrifying Tense Longing from Taking Place**. 88p. $9.95.
- ❏ Seaton, Peter. **The Son Master**. 64p. $5.
- ❏ Sherry, James. **Popular Fiction**. 84p. $6.
- ❏ Silliman, Ron. **The New Sentence**. 200p. $10.
- ❏ Silliman, Ron. **N/O**. 112p. $10.95.
- ❏ Smith, Rod. **Music or Honesty**. 96p. $12.95
- ❏ Smith, Rod. **Protective Immediacy**. 96p. $9.95
- ❏ Stefans, Brian Kim. **Free Space Comix**. 96p. $9.95
- ❏ Tarkos, Christophe. **Ma Langue est Poétique—Selected Works**. 96p. $12.95.
- ❏ Templeton, Fiona. **Cells of Release**. 128p. with photographs. $13.95.
- ❏ Templeton, Fiona. **YOU—The City**. 150p. $11.95.
- ❏ Torres, Edwin. **The All-Union Day of the Shock Worker**. 112 p. $10.95.
- ❏ Ward, Diane. **Human Ceiling**. 80p. $8.95.
- ❏ Ward, Diane. **Relation**. 64p. $7.50.
- ❏ Watson, Craig. **Free Will**. 80p. $9.95.
- ❏ Watten, Barrett. **Progress**. 122p. $7.50.
- ❏ Weiner, Hannah. **We Speak Silent**. 76 p. $9.95
- ❏ Wolsak, Lissa. **Pen Chants**. 80p. $9.95.
- ❏ Yasusada, Araki. **Doubled Flowering: From the Notebooks of Araki Yasusada**. 272p. $14.95.

ROOF BOOKS
are published by
Segue Foundation, 300 Bowery, New York, NY 10012
Visit our website at **segue.org**

ROOF BOOKS are distributed by
SMALL PRESS DISTRIBUTION
1341 Seventh Avenue, Berkeley, CA. 94710-1403.
Phone orders: 800-869-7553
spdbooks.org